JULIUS CAESAR

Ruler of the Roman World

Zachary Kent

Enslow Publishers, Inc.

40 Industrial Road   PO Box 38
Box 398   Aldershot
Berkeley Heights, NJ 07922   Hants GU12 6BP
USA   UK

http://www.enslow.com

Library of Congress Cataloging-in-Publication Data

Kent, Zachary.
    Julius Caesar : ruler of the Roman world / Zachary Kent.
       p. cm. — (Rulers of the ancient world)
    Includes bibliographical references.
    ISBN 0-7660-2563-2
    1. Caesar, Julius—Juvenile literature. 2. Heads of state—Rome—Biography—Juvenile
literature. 3. Generals—Rome—Biography—Juvenile literature. 4. Rome—History—
Republic, 265–30 B.C.—Juvenile literature. I. Title. II. Series.
    DG261.K46 2006
    937'.05'092—dc22

                             2005022485

Printed in the United States of America

10 9 8 7 6 5 4 3 2 1

To Our Readers:
We have done our best to make sure that all Internet Addresses in this book were active and
appropriate when we went to press. However, the author and publisher have no control over and
assume no liability for the material available on those Internet sites or on other Web sites they may
link to. Any comments or suggestions can be sent by e-mail to comments@enslow.com or to the
address on the back cover.

Illustration Credits: © The British Library/The Image Works, p. 13; © The British
Museum/Topham-HIP/The Image Works, p. 141; The British Museum/HIP/The Image Works,
p. 138; Clipart.com, design at the top of pp. 5, 10, 20, 36, 50, 63, 77, 87, 113, 124, 135, and image on
p. 6; © Corel Corporation, pp. 1, 107; The Library of Congress, pp. 4, 8, 115, 131; Enslow
Publishers, Inc., pp. 22–23; © Mary Evans Picture Library/The Image Works, p. 68.

Subhead Illustrations: Clipart.com

Cover Illustration: © Corel Corporation

CONTENTS

Julius Caesar

CROSSING THE RUBICON

The gray light of dawn crept through the leafless trees on January 10, 49 B.C. Several Roman army officers were gathered near a little bridge on the north bank of the Rubicon River. The Rubicon marked the border between the Roman province of Cisalpine Gaul and, to the south, the rest of the Roman Republic. Among the soldiers on that wintry morning stood a tall, dark-eyed, dignified man. He wore the red cloak of a general. The officers around him respectfully waited for him to speak. Fifty-year-old Julius Caesar silently gazed southward across the Rubicon. The little river was not wide, and it was not deep. But crossing it presented Caesar with the most difficult decision of his life.

CHALLENGED BY THE ROMAN SENATE

For the past nine years, Julius Caesar had been the governor of Cisalpine Gaul, as well as two other Roman provinces. His term of office was near its end. Now he wanted to return to Rome, the capital city. He wanted to run for the highest office the Roman Republic offered.

The Senate was the main lawmaking body of Rome.

He wished to win election as a consul for the year 48 B.C. Roman governors commanded legions of soldiers in order to keep peace in their provinces. While serving as governor, Caesar had used his armies to conquer all of Gaul. Gaul was a region that included much of present-day France and Belgium. Caesar's conquest of Gaul was as great a military feat as any in all of Rome's entire history. Caesar had forced the surrender of as many as eight hundred cities and three hundred Gallic tribes. His political enemies in Rome were jealous of his success and fearful of his power. For years, they had tried to find a way to ruin him.

Caesar had served as Roman consul once before in 59 B.C. During his year in office, he had trampled ruthlessly on the rights and powers of the Roman Senate. He had done so in order to get new laws passed. Many senators worried that if elected consul again, Caesar would behave the same way. These senators decided on a plan. Before he could offer himself as a candidate, the Senate demanded Caesar give up command of his army. Caesar guessed his enemies wished to see him arrested. He believed they wanted to have him brought to trial for crimes he may have committed during his first consulship.

A Difficult Choice

Caesar wrestled with a tremendous decision. For nine years he had been fighting bloody wars to gain glory for Rome. Now the Roman Senate insisted that if he did not surrender his command he would be defying the Republic. Caesar continued to stare across the Rubicon River. If he crossed the water, it would be against the Senate's will. Marching into Roman Italy at the head of his troops would be an act of treason. It would spark a civil war. However, if he surrendered to the demands of the Senate, his career as a politician and general almost surely would end. If condemned by trial, he might even face a death sentence.

Caesar stared across the icy river and thought. His friend Asinius Pollio recorded the scene. Caesar realized "how much misfortune the crossing would bring to all men."[1] Many times during his life, Caesar had risked his future and succeeded. Now he had to make another choice. "Even now we can still retreat," he admitted to his officers. "But once we cross this little bridge, everything will have to be settled by [force]."[2]

"The Die Is Cast"

Julius Caesar was a man of great intellect. The ancient Roman writer Pliny the Elder described him as a man "gifted with mental powers. . . . I will not speak here of his energy . . . or of his . . . ability to [understand] everything under the sun, but of the . . . fiery quickness of his mind."[3] As a politician and general, Caesar had often shown he could be ruthless, clever, determined, and bold. Already he had made himself one of the most powerful people in the strongest nation the world had ever seen. Ambition and pride would not allow him to give up his hard-earned position.

At last, Caesar made his fateful decision. He turned to his waiting officers. "The die is cast," he declared.[4]

When Caesar crossed the Rubicon, he made it very clear that he intended to invade Italy.

By this, he meant that he had made his decision. Having spoken, Caesar led his officers across the river and single-handedly plunged Rome into bloody civil war. Ever since, the saying "to cross the Rubicon" has meant to make a serious decision that cannot be changed. The choice Julius Caesar made on that winter morning in 49 B.C. would affect the Roman world forever.

2

A ROMAN CHILDHOOD

According to legend, Rome was founded in 753 B.C. in the Etruscan region of present-day central Italy. Through the next two centuries, Etruscan kings ruled Rome. Around 510–509 B.C., the last Etruscan king was overthrown. Rome's nobles founded a democratic form of government. The people voted for their leaders. This marked the start of the Roman Republic.

The highest officers of the Roman Republic were its two consuls. Two new consuls were elected to serve each year. To hold the office of consul was the greatest honor a Roman citizen could win. The two consuls kept order over the nobles seated in the Roman Senate. It was in the Senate that bills for new laws were offered and discussed. Once the Senate had agreed on a new bill, it was sent to the Assembly of the People. The Assembly was made up of common citizens. It was the Assembly alone that had the power to veto the bill or approve it and make it a law.

BUILDING AN EMPIRE

By 266 B.C., Rome controlled the entire Italian peninsula below the Po River. During the next one hundred thirty years, the Romans successfully battled against the Phoenician empire of Carthage in three wars. Roman armies defeated Carthage during what is called the First Punic War (264–261 B.C.). As a result, Rome took control of the islands of Sicily, Sardinia, and Corsica in the Mediterranean Sea. In the Second Punic War (218–202 B.C.), the great Carthaginian general Hannibal invaded Italy. Hannibal crossed the snowy Alps with an army that included elephants. In Italy, Hannibal fought hard and well, but at last his army was defeated. As a result of that war, Rome took control of most of the Iberian peninsula (present-day Spain and Portugal). Two new provinces called Nearer and Further Spain became part of the growing Roman Empire. Then, in 146 B.C., Rome invaded and destroyed Carthage itself. Rome renamed its newest province Africa (much of present-day Tunisia).

Rome extended its power in other directions as well. By 120 B.C., Roman armies had conquered and established provinces in Macedonia, Achaia (present-day Greece), Illyricum (the Balkan coast, including parts of Croatia, Bosnia, and Montenegro), Asia (western Turkey), Cilicia (southern Turkey), and Transalpine Gaul (the south coast of modern France).

By 100 B.C., the Roman Republic had existed for more than four hundred years. Rome had become the largest city in the world, a center of trade and culture. Nearly one million people crowded Rome's narrow streets. Rome ruled all of the Mediterranean world. King Mithridates fought to keep his kingdom on the Black Sea independent of Rome. Mithridates bitterly remarked,

"The Romans have constantly had the same cause . . . desire for empire and wealth."[1]

PATRICIAN POWER

Rome's citizens had created a more democratic government. The Assembly of the People elected government officers and passed the laws. In addition, each year, Rome's common people, the plebeians, elected ten tribunes. These tribunes had the power to protect public interests. A single tribune could use his veto and prevent a new law from passing.

In truth, however, most of the power in Rome was possessed by a few families. Members of Rome's noble class, the patricians, sat in most of the Senate's seats. Every member of the Senate had held an important government office at one time. It was to the Senate that all proposed new laws were first brought for discussion. The Roman historian Sallust remarked, "Whatever appears desirable, they seize and [make] their own, and transform their will and pleasure into their law . . ."[2] It was the Senate that decided Rome's foreign policy, including declaring wars and making peace treaties. Most government officeholders performed their duties under orders from the Senate. It was, therefore, the Senate that truly controlled Rome.

A NOBLE BIRTH

Gaius Julius Caesar was born on July 12, 100 B.C. The baby's father, the elder Gaius Julius Caesar, was a member of Rome's Julii family. The Julii were one of Rome's most ancient and noble families. Caesar's mother, Aurelia, was a member of another noble family, the Aurelii Cottae. Her father, Lucius Aurelius Cotta, and three of her cousins had all served as consuls. The new baby also had two sisters. They were named Julia Major and Julia Minor (meaning in Latin, Julia the

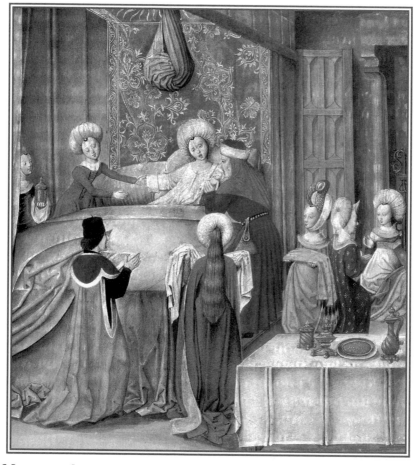

Many people attended to Julius Caesar's mother during his birth. This depiction of Caesar's birth was painted during a time called the Renaissance (c. 1300–1600), and the artist painted the people wearing Renaissance dress.

Elder and Julia the Younger). It was Roman custom to name all daughters after their father's family.

It was clear the child's family had a long and respected history. But at the time of his birth, the most important of all family relations was his Uncle Gaius Marius. Married into the Julii family, Marius ranked among Rome's greatest generals. A few years earlier, two huge German tribes, the Cimbri and the Teutoni, had threatened Italy with invasion. Marius had defeated them both. To give his troops fighting spirit, Marius had made them a promise. They would be rewarded with free plots of land to farm. After the wars, he used his power and influence to keep his promise. As a result, these soldiers felt more loyalty to Marius than they did to the Roman Republic. With the backing of his troops, Marius was elected consul four years in a row. In 100 B.C., he was serving his sixth term as consul. It was Marius who had shown the value of military support to Roman politicians.

NOBLE SCHOOLING

At birth, a golden good-luck charm (the bulla) would have been hung around the baby Caesar's neck. This was a Roman tradition with baby boys. It was also Roman custom that the boy would remain under his mother's care until he was seven years old. At home, the little boy was most likely taught about the many gods in the Roman religion. Each dawn, the son of a noble stood and watched his father's daily ceremony. A religious Roman would raise his right hand to his lips and respectfully turn in a circle. Then he would toss a piece of salted cake into the fireplace. This was an offering to Vesta, the Roman goddess of hearth and home.

Much of young Julius Caesar's education was provided by a private tutor. He learned reading and writing in the Roman language, Latin. He also learned ancient Greek, the language of scholars. Caesar's tutor for a time was Marcus Antonius Gnipho, an educated former slave. The Roman biographer Suetonius called Gnipho "a man of great talent, of unexampled powers of memory. . . . kindly and good-natured."[3] The typical Roman student practiced reading aloud. He recited the alphabet forward and backward in both Latin and Greek. He probably balanced across his knees a board with a wax film covering it. Into the wax he could practice writing letters with a metal or wooden needle (a stylus). To learn arithmetic, he could count numbers with his finger in a tray of sand or push the wooden beads of an abacus back and forth.

For physical exercise, Rome's noble children enjoyed sports. These often took place on the Campus Martius, just outside the city gates. "This is a . . . large field," described the ancient scholar Strabo, "on which an enormous number of chariots and horses can race . . . and . . . people can daily play ball games and practice discus-throwing and wrestling."[4] Sword practice and horseback riding were also popular sports. Although a thin and sickly child, Caesar worked hard to strengthen his body. "He had been an expert rider from his childhood," Greek biographer Plutarch later revealed, "for it was usual with him to sit with his hands joined together behind his back, and so to put his horse to its full speed."[5]

In His Father's Footsteps

Among Roman nobles, a boy's father took over control of his education when he reached the age of seven. The son would often join his father on his travels, observing everything he did. Young Julius Caesar probably watched his father's business dealings. He probably listened during adult discussions. He very likely went with his father to the Forum in Rome. The Forum was the city's central marketplace. In Rome, the Forum was where the Assembly met and where public speeches were made. Noble children were also permitted to accompany their fathers to the Senate. Surely young Caesar stood at the open Senate doors and listened to the debates.

Living in Rome must have made a great impression on the boy. All over the city stood marble statues of Rome's great generals and politicians. In the Forum, in temples, and in the public gardens, one could see Etruscan and Greek sculptures and paintings. Along the city streets, merchants bought and sold goods from all over the known world. To a Roman boy, Rome would seem like the center of the universe. He only had to decide what place he would take in it.

Young Caesar's father had already served as a quaestor, a treasury official. When the boy was nine years old, his father was elected to an even higher office, praetor. A praetor served as a judge in arguments between Romans and noncitizens. Caesar's father took office on January 1, 92 B.C. Each morning, he left home with six lictors (government attendants) going before him. The lictors carried bundles of birch sticks tied with red cords (the fasces). Fasces were the symbols of a man's important office. By tradition, the son followed between the last lictor and his father. It was a public show of his desire to follow in his father's footsteps through life. Caesar's father served a one-year term as a praetor. Then, the Senate chose him to become governor of the Roman province of Asia for one year. A governorship was the high reward for praetors who had shown good service.

CIVIL WAR IN ROME

In 90 B.C., when Julius Caesar was ten, civil war broke out in Rome. Mithridates, king of Pontus on the Black Sea, had invaded the province of Asia. This happened after Caesar's father had returned to Rome. At first, the Senate named Consul Lucius Cornelius Sulla to command Rome's armies in this war. Then, Caesar's uncle, seventy-year-old General Marius, persuaded Senate supporters to name him commander instead. Deeply insulted, Sulla marched his assembled soldiers into Rome in order to overturn the Senate's decision. Never before had armed troops entered the city. Marius called upon citizens and slaves to halt Sulla's advance through the city gates. All around Caesar's house, unarmed Romans threw stones and tiles from the roofs down on Sulla's troops. Bloody fighting left Rome's streets filled with dead.

At last, Marius was forced to flee to Africa. Sulla made himself dictator of Rome. Soon, Sulla left Italy to fight his war with Mithridates. In time, the Senate invited Marius and his political ally Lucius Cornelius Cinna to return to Rome. In 87 B.C., Marius and Cinna marched into the city. They killed hundreds of Sulla's supporters and sold their properties. The Senate elected Marius consul for 86 B.C., but the old general died shortly after taking office. For the moment, Cinna and his supporters were left in control of Rome. Cinna was elected consul three years in a row.

PUTTING ON THE TOGA

Rome had suffered several years of civil war and political unrest. During this time, Julius Caesar reached his early teenage years. When Caesar was fourteen, friends of his Uncle Marius arranged for him to enter training as a Flamen Dialis. A Flamen Dialis was a priest of the Temple of Jupiter. These priests oversaw the monthly animal sacrifices at the temple. Their solemn words started each year's grape harvest. They performed many other sacred duties as well. It would take as long as three years for young Caesar to learn all he needed to know.

When he reached the age of fifteen, Caesar at last removed his bulla, his baby's charm. He draped his body in the loose cloth of a toga. He had officially become a man. His father took him to the Forum. He was presented as an adult to the Roman public. It was not long after this that a messenger brought tragic news. His father suddenly had died while on a visit to the city of Pisa. The cause of his death is unknown.

When she learned of her husband's death, Aurelia put out the fire in the hearth. She placed a cypress branch outside the door of the house. When her husband's body arrived, she had it washed and laid out for his funeral. At last, she put a coin under the dead man's tongue. This was to pay the legendary ferryman to carry the body across the River Styx into the afterworld. All of this was done according to Roman custom.[6]

3

THE YOUNG PATRICIAN

The death of his father left young Julius Caesar the head of the Julii family. It was his responsibility now to win honor for the family name. Caesar had grown tall and slim. He tried to bring attention to himself in the style of his clothes. He often wore a loose belt tied around his middle. His tunics were designed so that the sleeves had fringes that reached to his wrists. This was a fancy and unusual style. The boy had also become vain about his handsome looks. He wore his hair perfumed and carefully combed. Sometimes he even had a servant pluck his eyebrows.[1]

A ROMAN MARRIAGE

It was not strange for teenagers to marry in Roman times. The consul Cinna recognized the political value of marrying his daughter to the nephew of the great general Marius. In 84 B.C., Cinna discussed such a marriage with sixteen-year-old Caesar. Caesar was already engaged at the time. He felt no romantic interest in Cinna's daughter, Cornelia. But he was full of political ambition.

Caesar wanted to improve his standing in Rome. He broke his engagement and agreed to marry fourteen-year-old Cornelia.

On their wedding day, ten witnesses from ten of Rome's most noble families watched the ceremony. The marriage contract was solemnly signed. Caesar and Cornelia exchanged rings. Then they made an offering to the gods of fruits and a slice of cake. After the religious sacrifice of an ox, the newlyweds and their guests attended a dinner at Cinna's mansion. The marriage of the two noble families was recognized as a major social event in Rome.

Within the next year, Cornelia and Caesar had a baby daughter. Of course, she was named Julia, because she was the daughter of a Julii. Caesar most probably followed the Roman custom of accepting his fatherhood. He lifted the newborn baby from the floor and into the air for all to see. He loved his daughter dearly. As she grew, she always remained one of the true delights of his life.

SULLA'S RETURN

In 82 B.C., General Sulla made peace with Mithridates in Asia. He determined he would return to Rome and seek revenge on his enemy Cinna. In time, he landed his army in Italy. Cinna planned to escape to Greece and renew the civil war. However, on his journey, the soldiers with him mutinied. In Ancona, Italy, Cinna was assassinated. Young Caesar had lost his father-in-law.

By the end of October 82 B.C., Sulla's army reached the outskirts of Rome. Sulla's moment for revenge had

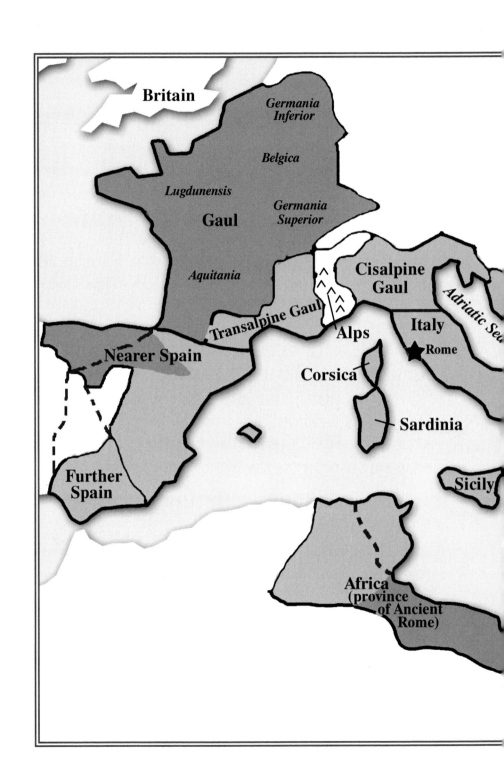

Britain

Germania
Inferior

Belgica

Lugdunensis

Germania
Superior

Gaul

Aquitania

Cisalpine
Gaul

Adriatic Sea

Transalpine Gaul

Alps

Italy

Nearer Spain

Rome

Corsica

Sardinia

Further
Spain

Sicily

Africa
(province
of Ancient
Rome)

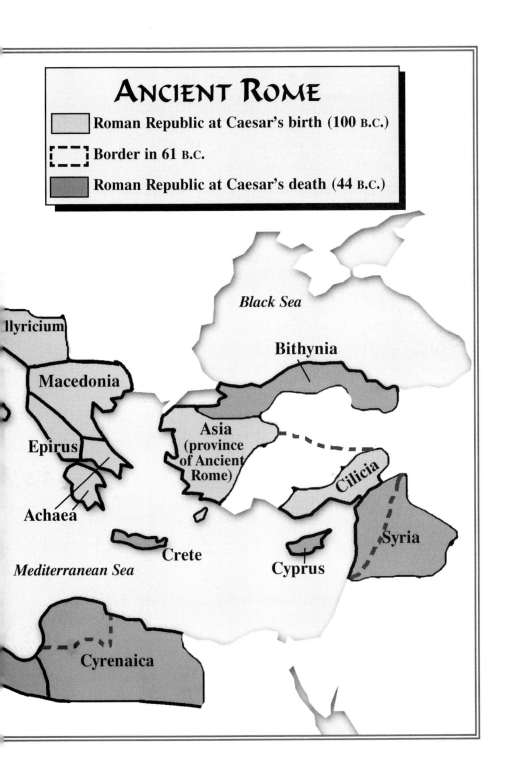

ANCIENT ROME

Roman Republic at Caesar's birth (100 B.C.)

Border in 61 B.C.

Roman Republic at Caesar's death (44 B.C.)

Black Sea

Illyricium

Bithynia

Macedonia

Epirus

Asia
(province
of Ancient
Rome)

Achaea

Cilicia

Crete

Syria

Cyprus

Mediterranean Sea

Cyrenaica

arrived. He immediately announced that no laws or elections decided upon while he had been away should be honored or obeyed. This announcement cost Caesar his position as a student priest of Jupiter. In addition, on November 1, 82 B.C., Sulla ordered the murders of six thousand political enemies captured the night before. Army officers loyal to Cinna were beheaded. Sulla ordered the tomb of Marius opened. His troops dumped the bones of that old enemy into a nearby river. A nephew of Marius, the praetor Gratidianus, suffered an especially gruesome fate. First, Sulla's men beat him in the streets and broke his arms and legs with sticks. Next, they sliced off his ears and ripped his tongue out of his mouth. Then they gouged out his eyes. While the tortured man was still breathing, they finally cut off his head.

Julius Caesar was lucky to escape a similar fate. Sulla called the eighteen year old to stand before him. As a nephew of Marius and Cinna's son-in-law, Sulla considered Caesar a dangerous man. Rather than having him killed, however, Sulla demanded that Caesar end his relationship with Cinna's family. He must divorce his wife, Cornelia.

This was more than a proud young man like Caesar could bear. Bravely, he refused to divorce his wife. In fear of his life, Caesar fled Rome on horseback. He escaped into the mountains east of the city. For a time, he shifted from one hiding place to another. At last, he fell seriously ill with malaria. Sulla's troops found him and took him prisoner.

He was now at Sulla's mercy. Yet Caesar's life was spared. It is believed by many historians that Caesar's mother and members of her noble family paid bribes and begged Sulla to pardon him. Sulla was tired of all the bloodshed in Rome. He finally agreed to do what Caesar's family wanted. But he guessed that Caesar would one day be troublesome. It is said Sulla told Caesar's rescuers, "Have your way and take him. Only bear in mind that the man you are so eager to save will one day deal the death blow to the aristocracy . . . for in this Caesar there is more than one Marius."[2]

DUTY IN ASIA

Caesar realized it was dangerous for him to remain in Rome. Luckily, the new governor of Asia, Marcus Thermus, invited Caesar to join his staff. In 80 B.C., Caesar boarded a ship bound for the Asian city of Ephesus. When he landed, Caesar discovered that Rome's Asian province was not totally at peace. Mitylene, a town on the coastal island of Lesbos, was in revolt. Governor Thermus chose Caesar to go on a military mission. Caesar was sent to King Nicomedes of Bithynia, on the southern coast of the Black Sea. It was Caesar's mission to persuade Nicomedes to lend his fleet of warships to Rome. When Caesar presented himself, Nicomedes found him very charming.

Caesar succeeded in borrowing Nicomedes' fleet. He sailed with it to Lesbos and joined in the attack on Mytilene. In combat, Caesar proved himself an able soldier. In the middle of the fight, he rescued a comrade. For his bravery, he was awarded the "citizen's crown." This was a wreath of oak leaves that he was allowed to wear on public occasions for the rest of his life. It was a high honor. Whenever he appeared wearing the wreath it was expected all spectators, including senators, would rise to their feet to salute him.

Following the surrender of Mytilene, Caesar journeyed to the Roman province of Cilicia (present-day southeastern Turkey). There he served on the staff of Governor Servilius Vatia. It was in Cilicia that Caesar learned that Sulla had died. The days of Sulla's dictatorship were over. Rome's senators had finally regained control of the Republic. Caesar decided immediately to return home.

PUBLIC PROSECUTOR

Twenty-three-year-old Caesar had served well in Asia and Cilicia, but he wished to accomplish much more. According to Roman law, no important government office could be held by anyone under the age of thirty. Caesar searched for some way to gain notice in the meantime. In Rome, lawyers could not charge fees. They performed their work for free as a public service. But Caesar realized lawyers could win public attention by bringing criminals to trial.

Trials took place in the Forum, where crowds of people gathered daily to watch and listen. After returning to Rome in 77 B.C., Caesar prosecuted Gnaeus Cornelius Dolabella. It was charged that Dolabella had stolen money while serving as Sulla's governor of Macedonia. Gaius Aurelius Cotta and Quintus Hortensius were the lawyers who defended Dolabella.

They ranked among the best public speakers in all of Rome. Hortensius in particular was famous for his skills. It was said that actors attended his trials in order to study his gestures.

The jury at Dolabella's trial was made up of Roman senators. Many of the senators were friends of the accused. Only months before, the Senate had awarded Dolabella a "triumph," a grand parade. This was to honor his military success while governor of Macedonia. In the end, Caesar lost his case. But Dollabella's trial helped Caesar establish a reputation as a brilliant public speaker. So did another trial the next year in 76 B.C. This time, Caesar prosecuted Gaius Antonius Hybrida. He was another of Sulla's men who was said to have stolen money from the Greeks. Again, Caesar lost, but he had spoken well and won more admirers. According to the ancient biographer Plutarch, in Caesar's displays as a public speaker, he won "great credit and favor" among common Romans.[3]

CAPTURED BY PIRATES

Caesar was making progress, but he believed his public speaking skills could be improved. In 75 B.C., he decided to journey to the Greek island of Rhodes. There, he planned to study the art of public speaking with the famous Greek teacher Apollonius Molon.

It was during the voyage to Rhodes that Caesar was captured by pirates near the island of Pharmacussa. The pirates demanded a ransom of twenty talents for their noble prisoner (about one thousand pounds of silver).

Caesar proudly announced he was worth much more than that. He offered them fifty talents. His fellow travelers were sent on to Rhodes to collect the money.

Caesar remained in the pirate camp with his personal doctor and two servants. He was a prisoner, but the pirates treated him with friendliness. "For thirty-eight days," Plutarch tells us, "with all the freedom in the world, he amused himself with joining in their exercises and games, as if they had not been his keepers; but his guards."[4] At times, Caesar watched the pirates practice their swordsmanship. He laughed at their clumsiness. When they wrestled, he took part in the fun. When they went swimming, he stripped down and dove in, too. To fill hours of boredom, he wrote poems, which he read aloud to the pirates. Often, he jokingly warned them of what he would do when he was free again. He would hunt them down and see them executed.

At last, the ransom was paid, and the pirates set Caesar free. He immediately journeyed to Miletus and took command of the ships in the harbor. He intended to keep his promise. He "went in pursuit of the pirates," explained Plutarch, "whom he surprised with their ships still stationed at the island, and took most of them."[5]

Most of the pirates who had kidnapped Caesar were now his prisoners. He shipped them to prison and eventually ordered them to be crucified. Being nailed alive to a wooden cross was the customary execution for criminals who were not Roman citizens. Since the pirates had been friendly, though, Caesar decided to spare them the slow painful death of the cross. As the writer

Suetonius later revealed, "He commanded that their throats be first cut, and then to be crucified."[6]

SERVICE ON RHODES

Caesar finally arrived on the island of Rhodes. Soon after his arrival, he learned that King Mithridates had invaded Bithynia. Caesar had barely begun his public speaking studies when he crossed the water to Asia to join the war. Although only a low-ranking officer, he helped raise volunteers to drive out the invaders. On the mainland, fifty miles east of Ephesus, his soldiers fought an enemy force and defeated it.

At the end of 74 B.C., twenty-six-year-old Caesar received news from Rome. He had been elected into the college of the pontifices. This was a religious position higher than Flamen Dialis. Rome's fifteen pontifices were the highest religious authority in the entire Republic. Caesar's mother, Aurelia, had used her family influence to win him the position. He immediately boarded a ship and started the journey to Rome.

THE SLAVE REVOLT OF SPARTACUS

"Show me a slave," an old Roman proverb claimed, "and I'll show you an enemy."[7] Throughout Italy, about one third of the population were foreigners enslaved during Rome's many wars. In the summer of 73 B.C., while traveling to Rome, Caesar learned of a slave revolt. About seventy slaves had escaped from a gladiator school. It was located in the province of Campania just south of Rome. Gladiators were slaves trained to fight with weapons for Roman entertainment. The slave revolt eventually attracted as many as seventy thousand rebellious slaves. Their leader was the gladiator Spartacus. He molded the slave mob into a dangerous army that marched north toward the Alps. Then they moved south again, destroying farms, burning homes, and killing Roman citizens.

At the end of 72 B.C., after more than a year of panic, the Roman Senate appointed Marcus Licinius Crassus to command the war against Spartacus. Crassus was the richest man in all of Rome. Romans told stories about his wise business sense. When buildings caught fire in Rome, Crassus cheaply bought them from their owners while they were still burning. As soon as he had made a deal, his slaves formed bucket brigades and put the fires out, saving the buildings. Other times, he let the buildings burn. Then he ordered his team of five hundred laborers and architects to erect a new building on the site. "As a result, a major part of Rome became his property," Plutarch later remarked.[8] In his writings, Plutarch also revealed that Crassus "owned numerous silver mines and very valuable lands, together with the manpower to work them . . ."[9]

Crassus had once declared, "A man whose income is insufficient to support an army can never become a leading statesman."[10] In the face of the slave revolt, Crassus had announced his willingness to recruit new legions at his own expense. So, Crassus received the command. With as many as forty thousand soldiers, Crassus eventually cornered the slave army at the southernmost tip of Italy. To keep them trapped, he ordered the high wooden walls of a barricade built. It stretched from the east coast to the west coast. After three attempts, however, Spartacus broke out. The slave army fled northward. Crassus and his Roman troops finally caught up with them near the seacoast city of Brindisi. Spartacus and most of his slave army died in the battle that followed.

Crassus had hoped he would win high praise for saving the Republic. But Roman general Gnaeus Pompey stole much of his glory. Pompey had been a successful general for thirteen years. Once a follower of Sulla, his loyal troops called him "Pompey the Great."[11] In the summer of 71 B.C., Pompey and his army legions were returning from service in Spain. On the march, they happened upon five thousand slaves retreating from Spartacus' final defeat. Pompey's troops slaughtered them all. Pompey soon reported to the Senate that it was he who had finished off the slave revolt.

It enraged Crassus to learn that Pompey was receiving more praise than he deserved. Crassus had captured six thousand slaves in his last fight with Spartacus. Now, he ordered that they be crucified along the Appian Way. This was the busy cobblestone highway that connected Brindisi with Rome. For more than a hundred miles along the road, slaves were nailed to crosses. There was a cross at every forty yards' distance. In this grim manner, Crassus proclaimed his victory. In the end, both Pompey and Crassus were elected to serve as the consuls for the year 70 B.C.

FURTHER SPAIN

Upon his return from Rhodes, the Assembly of the People elected Caesar as one of the Republic's twenty-four military tribunes. Military tribunes had the duty of raising troops and sometimes serving as officers. As a military tribune, Caesar may have fought in the war against Spartacus. However, historians are uncertain of this. For a time, Caesar served in Greece on the staff of Governor Marcus Antonius.

In 69 B.C., the Assembly elected Caesar as one of the Republic's twenty quaestors. In Rome, quaestors supervised the Republic's treasury. In the provinces, they assisted governors. As symbols of their respected rank, quaestors wore red leather shoes and tunics with a broad purple stripe. Service as a quaestor would entitle thirty-year-old Caesar to lifetime membership in the Senate.

A DESIRE FOR GREATNESS

Caesar's friends in Spain one day got a glimpse of his desire for greatness. The story is told by Plutarch in his biography of Caesar:

> It is said that . . . when free from business in Spain after reading some part of the history of Alexander, he sat a great while very thoughtful, and at last burst out into tears. His friends were surprised, and asked him the reason of it. "Do you think," said he, "I have not just cause to weep, when I consider that Alexander at my age had conquered so many nations, and I have all this time done nothing that is memorable."[12]

At about this time, Caesar's Aunt Julia, the widow of General Marius, died. Caesar spoke publicly in the Forum at her funeral. Not long afterward, Caesar's own wife Cornelia suddenly died. They had been married for fifteen years. Caesar delivered a funeral speech in the Forum for her, too. Caesar's speeches won him more support among the people.

Caesar served his quaestorship in 69 B.C. in the province of Further Spain (southwestern Spain). As a quaestor, Caesar was assigned to conduct the courts held in Further Spain's major cities. As a judge, he decided such things as land boundaries and water rights and the return of escaped slaves. After serving about a year and a half, Caesar again journeyed home.

AMBITION

Caesar had achieved success, but he wanted even more. Upon arriving in Rome, he attempted to widen his social influence and gain money to support his political ambition. In 67 B.C., he married Pompeia, the granddaughter of his old enemy Sulla. Caesar felt no romantic interest in Pompeia. He simply recognized the importance of her family, one of the richest in Rome.

The most important man in Rome at the time remained Pompey. When pirate fleets raided Italy in 67 B.C., the Senate called upon Pompey to defeat them. In just three months, Pompey, in command of the Roman navy, hunted down the pirates. He made the entire Mediterranean Sea safe for Roman merchant ships. The Senate promptly asked Pompey to follow up this victory with another task. King Mithridates of Pontus remained unconquered after more than twenty years. Pompey marched off at the head of his legions on a new military campaign. Caesar openly threw his support behind Pompey to increase his own popularity with Roman commoners.

In 66 B.C., Caesar was elected curator of the Appian Way. As curator, it was Caesar's duty to repair and improve the important highway. While at the job, he learned engineering skills as a builder of roads and bridges. Travelers spoke highly of his work. If it made him more popular, the costs were not important to Caesar. While curator, Plutarch reports that Caesar spent "vast sums of his own money."[13]

In truth, Caesar began to go deeply into debt. He spent far too freely. He loved collecting jewels, fine vases, and lovely paintings. He also enjoyed surrounding himself with servants, and they were costly to feed and clothe. Money meant nothing to Caesar. A few years earlier, he had built himself an expensive country lakeside home outside of Rome. But he was not happy with how it looked. So he had it torn down and built a new one in its place.

AEDILE

In 66 B.C., Caesar campaigned and won election as an aedile for the coming year. It was his next step up the political ladder. Rome's aediles were responsible for the public baths, the distribution of grain to the poor, and the city water supply. Other duties included keeping the markets orderly and supervising the city's public entertainments. The writer Suetonius tells us that while aedile Caesar "beautified the Capitol also with fair open galleries built for temporary use during the public shows and plays."[14]

In September 65 B.C., Rome's aediles organized two weeks of games. Caesar carelessly went deeper into debt to make sure the games were amazing. Horse races and chariot races dazzled audiences at the Circus. Crowds cheered at boxing matches and mobbed arenas to watch lions and tigers in combat. Then Caesar announced additional games to honor the twentieth anniversary of his father's death. He borrowed money from wealthy Crassus in order to present an astonishing series of gladiatorial duels. Romans filled temporary bleachers in the Forum. They pressed shoulder to shoulder staring down from the roofs and galleries of the surrounding buildings. Suddenly a cry of amazement roared out as a long line of gladiators marched into view. "He provided such a number of gladiators," later declared Plutarch, "that he entertained the people with three hundred and twenty single combats . . ."[15] Caesar's activities as aedile made him talked about throughout the city. It seemed he would have many supporters in his quest for higher office.

4

SENATOR AND CONSUL

Early in 63 B.C., at the age of thirty-seven, Caesar ran for the office of pontifex maximus, high priest of the Roman religion. Becoming the Republic's high priest would be a lifelong, honored position. Caesar understood that the position of pontifex maximus would greatly advance his political career.

PONTIFEX MAXIMUS AND PRAETOR

The priests were the voters for the office, and Caesar's efforts to win included making gifts and paying large bribes. He borrowed heavily to pay for his campaign. On election day, his mother walked him to the door of their home. He kissed her and, according to the ancient historian Plutarch, explained, "Mother, today you will either see me as high priest or I will be heading into exile."[1] He knew that if he lost the election he would have to leave Rome to escape repaying his debts.

In the end, Caesar won the election. He now moved out of his simple home in the Subura section of Rome. He moved into the official residence of the pontifex maximus. This was a grand mansion on the Via Sacra in the center of the city. As pontifex maximus, Caesar was responsible for Rome's religious treasury and library. It was his duty to decide questions of sacred law and make judgments in religious courts. He also was expected to conduct many of Rome's animal sacrifices and religious celebrations.

In addition to performing religious duties, Caesar ran for the office of praetor in 63 B.C. Successfully elected, he had reached at last the highest office ever held by his father. Rome's eight praetors served as the Republic's highest judges.

THE CONSPIRACY OF CATILINE

Lucius Sergius Catilina, known today as Catiline, was a Roman politician who failed to win election as a consul in 63 B.C. Instead, famed public speaker Marcus Tullius Cicero won one of the two consulships in the election. Bitter about his defeat, Catiline developed a plot with his closest supporters. They would murder Cicero and seize power. Before they could act, however, their plot was discovered. Catiline was in the Etruria region of Italy organizing a rebel army. But on December 3, 63 B.C., five of the other leading plotters were arrested in Rome. Two days later, the Senate gathered to decide the fates of the five prisoners. Cicero exclaimed in the Senate that Catiline planned "to burn down the entire city and kill you all."[2] He demanded that the five captured plotters be executed immediately, without trial. Such an extreme idea was against Roman law.

It was then that Julius Caesar rose in the Senate. He asked for permission to speak. Before the Senate, Caesar declared that to execute the plotters without trial was against the long traditions of the Republic. Instead, he urged that the five plotters have all of their property taken from them. In addition, they should be imprisoned in towns outside of Rome. This seemed to be a harsh enough fate to Caesar. Many senators nodded at Caesar's well-spoken words.

After Caesar's speech, Senator Marcus Porcius Cato rose to be heard. Cato gave a violent speech condemning the prisoners. It changed the minds of many senators. At last, by custom, to show their votes, they rose one by one and went to stand next to Cato. It was soon clear the Senate had decided the five plotters should be executed. On Cicero's order, the five men were taken to the prison across from the Forum. Down in its deepest cell, the men were immediately strangled to death. By this time, the Senate had grown terribly excited. Even Caesar's life was threatened, because he had spoken on behalf of the plotters. Some senators shouted that Caesar was a member of Catiline's evil plot. That day, Caesar barely escaped the Senate alive.

Within weeks, the Senate sent a legion of troops against Catiline's rebel army. In January 62 B.C., the rebel force was completely destroyed in Etruria. Catiline died in the fighting, and all of his soldiers were slaughtered.[3]

Caesar had taken a risk in defending the Catiline plotters. But he had also been defending Roman law. As the days passed, many Romans praised Caesar's wisdom and bravery.

Pompey's Return

The general Pompey had been away from Rome for five years. After defeating Mithridates in Asia, at last Pompey landed at Brindisi, Italy, in December 62 B.C. When he reached Rome, the Senate announced plans to honor him with a triumph. It would be Pompey's third triumph. Already he had won wars in Africa and Spain. Now he could add more regions to his list of successes. He had made Mithridates' huge kingdom of Pontus part of the Roman Empire. He had also made Syria a new Roman province.

On September 28, 61 B.C., Pompey the Great rode in his third triumph through the streets of Rome. The entire city celebrated. Crowds cheered Pompey as a hero, as the horses of his chariot drew him onward.

Some people whispered that while Pompey was in Asia, Caesar had had a love affair with Pompey's wife Mucia. Pompey himself had heard these rumors. Upon his return to Rome, one of the first things Pompey did was divorce his wife. It was becoming clear to Pompey that he had a rival in Caesar, not only in love but also in politics.

Festival of the Bona Dea

After a year of service, each of Rome's eight praetors received a reward. The Senate named them governors of

Roman provinces. For the year 61 B.C., the Senate named Caesar governor of Further Spain. It was the same province in which he had served as a quaestor six years before. As he prepared to leave for Spain, Caesar became mixed up in a personal scandal.

The festival of the Bona Dea was celebrated at the end of every year in Rome. The Bona Dea, "The Good Goddess," was worshiped only by women. Only women were invited to attend a party in the house of an important government official. In this year, the festival took place in the home of Julius Caesar, praetor and high priest.

All went well on the night of the festival, until a wild young nobleman named Publius Clodius arrived. "Publius Clodius . . . was in love with Pompeia, Caesar's wife . . ." remarked Plutarch in his writings.[4] Clodius snuck into the Bona Dea celebration disguised in women's clothes. Before he could be alone with Caesar's wife, a servant discovered him and screamed. Clodius ran out of the house.

"In the morning, it was all about the town . . ." Plutarch later declared.[5] When he learned the story, Caesar's response was immediate. "Caesar's wife must be above suspicion," he proudly insisted.[6] He announced he would divorce Pompeia right away. After five years of marriage, Pompeia had not given Caesar any children. He longed to have a son. It is thought he used the Bona Dea scandal as an excuse to find himself a new wife.[7]

GOVERNOR OF FURTHER SPAIN

Caesar made hurried plans to leave Rome for Spain. By this time, he was so deeply in debt that he admitted that "he needed twenty-five million sesterces in order to have nothing at all."[8] The people who had loaned him money were hounding him for repayment. Some threatened him with prison. Wealthy Marcus Crassus realized the political value of having Caesar as a friend. Just before Caesar left for Spain, Crassus loaned Caesar more money. Twenty million sesterces could pay off most of Caesar's debts.

At last, Caesar set out on his journey. In crossing the Alps, he and his fellow travelers stopped at a humble little village. Some of the men questioned the value of such a poor place. In response, Caesar gravely declared, "I for my part would rather be the first man here than the second man in Rome."[9] In all things, Caesar's ambition demanded that he be most respected.

Caesar arrived in Further Spain and took up his duties as governor. Trouble plagued the Roman province. Large bands of thieves hid in the Lusitanian Mountains. Caesar demanded that these robbers stop their raids on the coastal towns of the province. When they refused, Caesar raised some five thousand new soldiers. They assembled with the two Roman legions already under his command. With energy and skill, Caesar marched against the Lusitanian raiders. Months of fighting saw the defeat of the lawless raiders. Caesar brought peace to the region and happily kept much of the robbers' treasure for himself.

A TRIUMPH OR AN ELECTION

Before the end of his term in office, Caesar hurried back to Rome. During the summer of 60 B.C., new elections were being held. Caesar wanted to run for consul. Arriving outside Rome, however, he discovered a new law had been passed. It demanded that all candidates for consul personally register their names before the July elections.

Caesar was faced with a problem. For his military success in Further Spain, the Senate had promised him a triumph. Such an important public honor suited Caesar's sense of vanity. However, by law, a general could not enter Rome until the day of his triumph. Clearly, he could not have both his parade and register his name to run for consul. Faced with an unhappy decision, Caesar finally chose to give up his claim to a triumph. He took off his general's cloak and entered Rome to record his name as a candidate for consul. To many Romans, Caesar had become a rising force in the Republic's politics. Cicero remarked that Caesar "has the wind in his sails just now."[10]

THE TRIUMVIRATE

In the contest for consuls in 60 B.C., Caesar had many supporters. Still he realized he could not win the election unless he spent lots of money on bribes. In a brilliant political move, he approached the two most powerful men in Rome. He suggested to Pompey and Crassus that they join him in a secret alliance. As a war hero, Pompey had the support of his thousands of army veterans. As Rome's richest citizen, Crassus had plenty of money to spend on the election. Through the years, Caesar himself had gained the support of huge numbers of the common people in Rome.

There would be benefits for all three men in such an alliance. They would have armed force, money, and Caesar's power as consul. Together, the three of them would be able to achieve whatever they wanted in the Republic. According to the historian Suetonius, they agreed "that nothing should be done or passed . . . that displeased any of them three."[11] The alliance of Caesar, Pompey, and Crassus would in time become known as "The Triumvirate," which meant a ruling group of three.

CAESAR'S ELECTION

In July 60 B.C., the election of Rome's two consuls was held. Roman citizens from distant Italian towns traveled into the city to vote. At dawn on election day, trumpets called the voters together near the Campus Martius. In the open field, an election official stood on a raised platform. He began the election by making a solemn prayer. Then he announced the names of the candidates. There were no election speeches. The citizens immediately lined up to vote. In order to vote, they entered temporary wooden booths. At each entrance, voting tablets were handed out. After writing the name of their candidate, citizens passed out of the booths one at a time. They crossed over a narrow bridge apart from their fellow voters. This insured that they could hand in their tablets without outside influences.

Voters were organized into "centuries," groups of one hundred. One by one, the members of the first century dropped their votes into the collection urn. The votes of the first century were counted and revealed immediately. Their decision was regarded as a fateful omen. The centuries that followed usually voted the same way. When a candidate had obtained a majority of votes, the counting stopped. In the 60 B.C. election, Caesar captured first place. He won an overwhelming vote of the centuries. Marcus Calpurnius Bibulus, who was Cato's son-in-law, won election as second consul.

THE NEW CONSUL

At dawn on New Year's Day, 59 B.C., slaves helped Julius Caesar dress in a purple robe. He left his mansion and climbed onto a chariot, as spectators waved and cheered. Twelve lictors carried fasces, the bundles of sticks that symbolized his new office as consul. The lictors walked ahead in single file. Caesar's mother, Aurelia; his daughter, Julia; relatives; and political supporters all joined the grand parade to the Capitol. At the Capitoline Hill, Caesar stepped from his chariot and climbed the steps leading to the Temple of Jupiter. There, he joined his fellow consul Bibulus. They publicly thanked the god Jupiter for protecting Rome during the previous year. Then they supervised the sacrifice of heifers (young cows). Inside the temple, Caesar made his first speech as consul. He called for peace and friendship among the senators. "[Caesar] would propose no measure," he announced, "which should not also be to their advantage."[12]

The fateful year of the consuls Gaius Julius Caesar and Marcus Calpurnius Bibulus had begun. The Senate met at once. Caesar held his first session as consul. He immediately introduced something new. He ordered that daily reports be published describing the business of the Senate and the Assembly of the People. This was the first time in Rome's history that this would be done regularly.

THE LAND BILL

Caesar's greatest enemy during his year as consul would be Marcus Cato. Cato strongly believed in Rome's republican values and traditions. Caesar's first business as consul was to offer a bill in the Senate. He wanted a new law to give away public land to Pompey's army veterans. Immediately, Cato rose from his seat and spoke out against the bill. Time passed, and still Cato kept talking. He would not give up the floor.

Caesar listened in frustration and growing anger. At last, he lost his temper. He ordered Cato arrested by Senate guards. Many senators shifted uneasily in their seats as Cato was led away to prison. This was not the way to run the Senate. Muttering and grumbling, dozens of senators began to leave. Caesar demanded to know why they were going. "Because I'd rather be with Cato in prison," one senator angrily replied, "than in the Senate House with you."[13] Furiously, Caesar realized he would have to back down. He ordered that Cato be released.

Abandoning the Senate-House altogether, Julius Caesar took his land bill directly into the Forum. Caesar knew the Assembly of the People could pass the bill without the advice of the Senate. In the Forum, Pompey and Crassus stood beside him as he addressed the gathered Assembly of the People. Already Rome had filled with Pompey's army veterans in answer to Pompey's call. One of Pompey's officers, Publius Vatinius, had organized the men into gangs. By using threats and violence, Vatinius' men soon controlled the city streets. Cato and Rome's other senators now understood the situation. Caesar, Pompey, and Crassus had secretly seized power.

Cato and Bibulus still tried to stop the passage of the land bill. When the day arrived for the Assembly's vote, Bibulus entered the Forum. As second consul, he claimed that he had seen unfavorable omens in the sky. As a result, no Assembly business could be conducted on that day. It was standard religious practice. Caesar quickly responded by giving a signal to Vatinius. Vatinius promptly set his men upon Bibulus. First they dumped a bucket of dung on the man's head. Then they threw him down the temple steps. Vatinius' men laughed aloud as Bibulus and Cato fled from the Forum. The Assembly passed the land bill by a unanimous vote. It seemed few Romans dared defy the wishes of Caesar, Pompey, and Crassus.

The Three-Headed Monster

There was no question that Caesar's methods as consul were illegal. But the Triumvirate was too strong for his

Senate enemies to resist. The passage of the land bill shamed and outraged Senate members. Cicero argued that Caesar's consulship was "the most scandalous in history, the most disgraceful and . . . hated by all sorts, classes, and ages of men."[14] The Roman writer Appian called the alliance among Caesar, Pompey, and Crassus the "three-headed monster."[15] The historian Dio Cassius later remarked, "Together they controlled the public business, granting to themselves or obtaining from one another what they desired . . ."[16]

To strengthen his position with Pompey, in April 59 B.C., Caesar arranged that the general marry his daughter, Julia. Pompey was forty-seven years old and Julia was only seventeen. Surprisingly, though, it would turn out to be a happy marriage.

Just days after the announcement of Julia's engagement to Pompey, Caesar made another announcement. He, too, would be marrying again. He had become engaged to eighteen-year-old Calpurnia, the daughter of wealthy nobleman Calpurnius Piso. After Caesar married Calpurnia, he arranged for her father to be elected as consul for the next year.

THE WILL OF THE GODS

The Romans believed that they could tell the future if they studied the organs of sacrificed animals. They believed in other omens as well. A sudden flight of birds, a thunderstorm, a streak of light across the sky (a meteor), or some other unusual happening all gave special warnings. As the days of 59 B.C. passed, Bibulus tried to prevent the passage of Senate and Assembly business. He continued to declare that he saw omens that warned against it. He proclaimed also that all of the remaining days of the year were to be public holidays. He tried to keep the Senate and the Assembly closed. Then he retired to his house and refused to appear in public. It was supposed no government actions could be taken unless Bibulus, as consul, took part.

All of these things were done in an effort to stop Caesar. But Caesar simply ignored Bibulus and conducted the government without him. "From that time forward," Roman biographer Suetonius remarked, "Caesar alone managed all the affairs of state . . ."[17]

In protest, most members refused to attend the Senate when Caesar was there. It did not matter to Caesar. With the support of Pompey and Crassus, he ran the government as he pleased. During his year in office, he often broke Senate rules and laws. Through the threat of force, he and his two partners silenced nearly all of their enemies.

GOVERNMENT BUSINESS

Loyal to the Triumvirate, Vatinius had been elected a tribune of the people. Caesar had Vatinius offer a bill approving everything Pompey had done while fighting in the east. The passage of this bill greatly enriched Pompey. Next, Caesar satisfied Crassus by arranging for a new tax law that brought Crassus huge profits. Not long afterwards, Caesar introduced a second land bill. It would provide public land in Campania (the Italian province south of Rome) to another twenty thousand of Pompey's veterans. It also gave land to Roman citizens with more than three children. This bill was also pushed through the Assembly of the People. In settling these lands, both Pompey and Caesar gained more influence and power.

As 59 B.C. drew to a close, Vatinius put forward another bill. It granted Caesar the governorship of two provinces, Cisalpine Gaul and neighboring Illyricum, after his term as consul. Caesar would be given a five-year term as governor instead of the normal two years. Before the year ended, the newly elected governor of Transalpine Gaul suddenly died. Pompey and Crassus insisted that Caesar be assigned this province, too.

Caesar had secured his future. He would be governor of three provinces. As governor, he would have a huge army at his command. In addition, he would be safe from his enemies. As long as he held government office, he could not be brought to trial for anything he had done while consul. That was Roman law. Once again, Caesar was having things his own way. "No one approves of what has taken place," remarked Cicero, "everyone complains . . . people all agree . . . but no one knows what to do. If we resist there will probably be bloodshed."[18]

Caesar had crushed the power of the Senate during his year in office. He had been successful because he had been ruthless. With the continued support of Pompey and Crassus, he believed nothing bad could happen to him. In fact, the future seemed to promise him continued good fortune and greatness.

5

PROVINCIAL GOVERNOR

At the start of March 58 B.C., forty-one-year-old Julius Caesar started a new chapter in his life. He was governor of three provinces. He was also the general of the legions in those provinces. As an army general, Caesar hoped to win fame as a warrior.

UNCONQUERED GAUL

Transalpine Gaul was one of Caesar's provinces. It lay beyond the high peaks of the Alps in present-day southern France. North of that province was a region unknown to most Romans. This was Gaul in what is today most of France and Belgium. It was a land of fertile soil and rich natural resources. Between 10 million and 15 million people lived in Gaul. They were organized into about three hundred separate tribes. Many Romans regarded the Gauls as barbarians. The Greek traveler Diodorus Siculus described the Gauls as "tall . . . and . . . terrifying in appearance, with deep-sounding and very harsh voices."[1] The men of Gaul did not wear togas. They dressed in strange woolen trousers, with plaid or checkered designs. Over their linen blouses, they wore cloaks fastened by bronze pins.

Unlike the Roman religion, the Druid religion of the Gauls held a strong belief in reincarnation. Caesar himself later wrote, "They . . . stress the belief that the soul does not die, but passes after death from one body to another; and they think that by this belief men are especially spurred on to courage, since the fear of death has been removed."[2] The Gauls were indeed warlike and seemed undefeatable. If Caesar could conquer Gaul, it would certainly bring him glory.

THE HELVETII MIGRATION

In March 58 B.C., just eight days after leaving Rome, Caesar arrived in Geneva in Transalpine Gaul. He had galloped on horseback as many as ninety miles in a single day. Caesar had been warned that many thousands of Helvetii had gathered on the banks of the Rhone River. They were camped across from the Roman garrison at Lake Geneva. The Helvetii were a fierce tribe. They normally lived in the mountain region between Germany and Gaul, present-day Switzerland.

Caesar had learned that the Helvetii had decided to march through Transalpine Gaul. They wanted to cross the Roman province in order to conquer and resettle on lands in western Gaul. "Considering their population and their reputation for war and bravery," Caesar described, "they felt that they had too small a territory . . ."[3]

Caesar believed the warlike Helvetii would destroy the countryside if allowed to pass through it. He quickly set his soldiers to work. They built a sixteen-foot-high wooden barricade. It stretched an amazing nineteen miles from Lake Geneva to the Jura Mountains. Caesar hoped this wooden wall would keep the Helvetii from carrying out their plan.

Leaders of the Helvetii soon came to meet with him. Caesar told them that "following the custom . . . of the Roman people, he could not grant anyone a right of way through the Province, and he made it clear that, if they tried to use force, he would stop them."[4] Already he had begun to enlist more soldiers.

As the days passed, Caesar learned that the Helvetii had decided upon another route into Gaul. With difficulty, they crossed through a narrow mountain pass and down through the territory of the Sequani tribe. Now they were in the Gallic region of the Aedui tribe. To feed themselves, they ruthlessly raided Aedui farmlands. The Aedui were allies of Rome. By treaty, Caesar had a responsibility to aid these defenseless people.

Caesar hurried his army forward. They marched day and night across the Alps. On a spring day in 58 B.C., he surprised the Helvetii as they were crossing the Saone River. Three quarters of the Helvetii had reached the west bank of the river. Caesar attacked the one quarter still on the east bank. His soldiers completely slaughtered them. Caesar later revealed that the few Helvetii survivors of the battle "took to flight and hid in the nearest woods."[5]

Caesar ordered a bridge quickly built across the river. In a single day, he crossed his entire army over to the west bank. The Helvetii were stunned at the speed with which Caesar had crossed. It had taken the Helvetii themselves twenty days to cross on rafts. For the next two weeks, the Romans marched after the Helvetii. Then Caesar realized he needed supplies. He directed his army to the Gallic town of Bibracte. The Helvetii seized this chance to attack.

Caesar prepared his men for battle. He ordered his horse and the horses of his officers led away to the rear. There would be no thought of retreat. He shouted encouragement to his troops, as the Helvetii charged upon them. He later wrote, "Hurling their javelins from their higher position, our soldiers easily broke up the mass formation of the enemy. Having thrown them into disorder, they drew their swords and made an attack upon them."[6]

The Helvetii fought hard. The battle raged all afternoon and into the night. At last, the Romans forced their enemy to fall back. After retreating for three days, the beaten Helvetii had had enough. A group of Helvetii leaders came to Caesar. They threw themselves at his feet and begged for peace.

Caesar ordered the Helvetii to return to their original territory. In Rome, citizens cheered the thrilling news of Caesar's victory. He had protected Transalpine Gaul and Rome's Aeduan ally. In his first campaign in the region of Gaul, Caesar had shown rare military skills.

GERMAN RAIDERS

After the Helvetii, Caesar fought a second enemy in 58 B.C. German raiders had crossed the Rhine River into

ROMAN SOLDIERS

A fully staffed Roman legion consisted of six thousand soldiers. The typical soldier wore a short-sleeved woolen tunic (blouse) that reached to his knees. Over this he usually wore heavy leather body armor to protect his chest and back. On his lower legs, he wore metal or leather shin guards. His helmet of leather or bronze had a stiff rising plume of horsehair to make him appear taller. On the march, soldiers carried up to sixty pounds of equipment. This included spare clothing, food rations, and a pot or pan for cooking. Most soldiers carried a gladius (a short double-edged sword). They also carried two metal-tipped wooden javelins (spears). Finally, every enlisted soldier marched with a scutum. This was a rectangular wooden shield that measured about two feet by four feet in size.

northern Gaul. They were commanded by Ariovistus, king of the Suebi tribe. Diviciacus, a leader of the Aeduans, came to Caesar. "You, Caesar," he requested, "by your own influence and that of your army . . . could . . . defend the whole of Gaul from . . . Ariovistus."[7] Caesar gladly grasped this opportunity to march farther into Gaul and gain more glory.

Caesar swiftly put his army into motion and moved against Ariovistus. Vesontio (present-day Besancon in Alsace, France) was the largest town of the Sequani tribe. Caesar kept his troops on the road night and day and reached the town before the raiding Germans.

Ariovistus finally agreed to talk with Caesar. The Roman general and the German king met on an open plain. Roman and German cavalry watched the meeting from a distance. Ariovistus remained fearless. He insisted that Caesar let the Germans do as they pleased in Gaul. Caesar replied that he was there to protect Rome's allies by order of the Senate. Before the talks could progress, the German horsemen attacked the Romans. Caesar returned safely to camp and reported what had happened. His soldiers, he later declared, "were inspired with a much greater enthusiasm and eagerness for battle."[8]

Caesar's troops had heard frightening talk from Gallic and Roman traders. The traders had exclaimed that the Germans were fearless giants and skilled warriors. They could strike terror into people simply with the keen stare of their blue eyes. Caesar boldly stated at a council of his officers, "I intend to execute at once what I might have put off to a more distant day . . ."[9] He would continue to press the enemy.

THE DEFEAT OF ARIOVISTUS

At last, Caesar positioned his army within fighting distance of the Germans. He expected them to attack. Yet, day after day, the Germans remained in camp. Finally, he questioned some prisoners and learned why. It was the habit among the Germans to wait for a battle omen. Women priests drew lots and used other methods to decide when it was best to fight. Caesar later wrote, "On this occasion they had declared that the Germans [would not] win if they fought before the new moon."[10] The German holy women had given Caesar the key to victory. He immediately ordered an attack. He would force the enemy to fight when they believed it would be bad luck. Roman officers brought the legions into battle formation. Trumpets sounded the signal to charge.

The Roman army rushed toward the enemy camp. The Germans hastily drew up a battle line arranged by tribes. These included the Harudes, Marcomani, Triboci, Vangiones, Nemetes, Sedusii, and Suebi. Behind their line, they placed their wagons and carts. Weeping German women stood on the wagons, begging husbands, sons, and brothers to protect them from the Romans.

Caesar later commented, "The enemy rushed forward so suddenly and swiftly that there was no time to hurl javelins at them."[11] The Romans dropped their javelins and drew their swords. In close, heavy combat, the Roman soldiers finally broke the German line. The Germans fled in total defeat. They retreated fifteen miles until stopped by the wide Rhine River. Some Germans escaped by swimming across the river, including Ariovistus. "Our cavalry," Caesar declared, "caught up with the rest and killed them."[12] At the end of the summer, Caesar encamped his troops in the Gallic region of the Sequani tribe. During his first six months as governor, Caesar had brutally defeated two major enemies, the Helvetii and the Germans. He had shown on the battlefield how foolish it was to challenge him.

FIGHTING THE NERVII

During the winter of 58–57 B.C., Caesar enlisted two more legions in Cisalpine Gaul (northern Italy). By spring, he had returned to Gaul. His entire army in Gaul now numbered some forty thousand men. During the winter, Caesar had received news. He noted that "all the Belgae were [plotting] against Rome."[13] The Belgian tribes, over three hundred thousand people, resented having Roman troops camped in Gaul.

Early in 57 B.C., Caesar marched to a Belgian stronghold at Suessiones (present-day Soissons). The Romans besieged the walled town. Some of his skilled soldiers built a mantlet, which was a roof-covered battering ram. Others shoveled dirt to build a ramp against the wall. Still more men constructed wooden siege towers to pull up the ramp. Soldiers inside these high, wheeled towers could safely fire arrows at the enemy. The defending Bellovaci tribe of the town were stunned by this advanced Roman technology. They soon surrendered. By early summer, most of the Belgian tribes had quit their fight.

One tribe, however, was determined to keep fighting. The Nervii, according to the writer Plutarch, were "the fiercest and most warlike people of all in those parts."[14] Caesar marched eight legions northeast toward the Nervii camp, which was in the forest beyond the Sambre River. One after another the Roman legions crossed the water. They began setting up camp on the top of a hill. The Nervii chose this moment to launch a sudden attack. Out of the woods, thousands of screaming warriors charged the Roman camp. Caesar later explained, "So short was the time, and so ready for battle was the spirit of the enemy that our men had no time . . . to put on their helmets . . ."[15]

Trumpeters grabbed their bugles. Soldiers tried to get into formation. The XIIth Legion was soon completely surrounded, and still more Nervii swarmed up the hill. Caesar saw that his army was in serious danger. He snatched a shield from a soldier for protection and rushed into the fray. He shouted orders and encouragement. "My arrival gave the troops fresh hope," he later claimed.[16]

Caesar ordered the VIIth Legion to shift position. Soon it was back to back with the XIIth Legion. The two legions were able to protect one another. Not a moment too soon, Roman relief finally arrived. Two fresh legions that had been traveling with the baggage wagons reached the battlefield. The Romans began to turn the tide. The Nervii still fought bravely. "When the first line had fallen," Caesar described, "the second took up position on the bodies of the fallen and went on fighting."[17]

At last, the few surviving Nervii retreated from their heaps of dead. Caesar later claimed that his troops had killed nearly sixty thousand men that day. The Nervii were nearly completely destroyed as a tribe.

THE ADUATUCI

Caesar fought one last battle in 57 B.C. Aduatuci warriors had been on the way to help the Nervii. But these Gauls arrived too late. The tribe took refuge in a walled town, which Caesar soon surrounded. Again Caesar's officers had mantlets constructed and siege towers on wheels built. Again Roman soldiers shoveled dirt, creating huge ramps against the town walls.

"When the enemy saw us building a siege-tower some distance away," Caesar noted, "they shouted down insults at us."[18] They refused to believe the Romans could move the large siege towers forward. When the Romans actually began rolling the towers toward the town, the enemy was shocked. They decided only a people favored by the gods could do such a thing. Before the attack could begin, they opened their gates and surrendered.

Caesar demanded the Aduatuci warriors give up all of their weapons. Some tribesmen, however, secretly kept their swords and spears. That night, they tried to fight their way out of the town. They rushed out of the gates and into the Roman camp. Caesar's troops were prepared for the attack. They let loose a rain of javelins and arrows. In the bloody fight, the Romans killed four thousand Aduatuci. The survivors retreated back into the town.

The next morning, the Romans used their battering rams to smash open the gates. Caesar made prisoners of everyone inside. Because they had dishonored their surrender terms, Caesar sold fifty-three thousand Aduatuci to the slave dealers who followed his army everywhere. These Gauls were marched in chains to the busy slave market in Rome. The sale of slaves brought Caesar much money. The slaves also gave Romans proof of his successes in Gaul.

While Caesar was conquering the northeastern region of Gaul, he sent General Publius Crassus to battle in the west. Publius Crassus was the son of wealthy Marcus Crassus. General Crassus discovered that the Gauls in the west had no desire to resist the Romans. Impressed by Caesar's victories, the Gauls along the coast (present-day Normandy and Brittany, France) submitted to Roman rule.

In two years, Caesar had crisscrossed Gaul. He had demonstrated Rome's military power by brutal example. Every tribe he had fought had been defeated. Romans were grateful for Caesar's astonishing success. In the fall of 57 B.C., the Senate granted Caesar a public thanksgiving period of fifteen days. No Roman general ever before had been granted such an honor. In 63 B.C., Pompey had only received ten days of public thanksgiving for his military victories.

CONFLICT IN ROME

Each winter, while governor, Caesar spent his time in Cisalpine Gaul in northern Italy. It was his province closest to Rome. From there, he could keep a closer watch on the political situation. In his winter camp, Caesar kept his secretaries, Oppius and Balbus, writing constantly. He sent advice and instructions to his Senate supporters. He paid out bribes and planned political strategy. Caesar had messengers riding back and forth to Rome all of the time.

In letters from Rome, Caesar learned alarming news that winter. The nobleman Publius Clodius was causing riots in the streets of the city. This was the same Clodius who had tried to sneak into the Bona Dea festival at Caesar's home. Now, he had organized gangs of thugs in Rome. His men swarmed over the city. Rome possessed no police force to keep the peace. It seemed Clodius wished to take power in Rome using the armed force of his mob.

Before the winter was over, another Roman, Titus Annius Milo, began to hire gangs of his own. Milo was a follower of Pompey. Milo brought armed men into the city from Pompey's country estates. He also purchased well-trained gladiator slaves to fight for him. Before long, the gangs of Clodius and Milo were battling for control of the streets. Cicero sadly declared, "The Tiber [River] was full of citizens' corpses, the public sewers were choked with them and the blood that streamed from the Forum had to be mopped up with sponges."[19]

This news from Rome greatly disturbed Caesar. But while serving as a governor, he was not legally permitted to return to Rome.

THE TRIUMVIRATE RENEWED

In the spring of 56 B.C., Caesar called for an emergency meeting with Pompey and Crassus. They met at the town of Luca in southern Cisalpine Gaul. Caesar was concerned about the future of the Triumvirate. The three men decided Crassus and Pompey should become consuls in 55 B.C. To ensure this, Caesar promised to send troops to Rome for the election. Their votes would help get Crassus and Pompey elected. In 49 B.C., when

Caesar's service as governor had ended, it was agreed that he would run for his second consulship.

Once in office, Pompey and Crassus promised they would pass a law granting Caesar the governorship of his three provinces for another five years. They would also fix their own appointments as future provincial governors. Pompey would go to Spain and Crassus to Syria for five-year terms. By renewing their alliance at Luca, the three men boldly expected to share the Roman Republic and fill government offices with their supporters. It was a masterful plan designed by Caesar.

Crassus and Pompey used the terror of Milo's gangs to win their elections as consuls in January 55 B.C. The night before the election, thugs attacked candidate Domitius Ahenobarbus and some of his supporters. A servant was killed, and Senator Cato received a wound in the arm. Brutal methods such as these, as well as the payment of bribes, allowed Pompey and Crassus to win the election.

Caesar once again controlled the political situation in Rome. His successes in Gaul had kept many of his political enemies silent and had won others to his side. Cicero, for one, recognized Caesar's growing power. "Can I," he asked his listeners in the Senate, "be the enemy of this man whose dispatches, whose fame, whose [messengers] fill my ears every day with fresh names of races, peoples, places?"[20]

6

GAULS, GERMANS, AND BRITONS

Caesar planned to visit his other province, Illyricum, in early 56 B.C. Before he could begin the journey, however, he received disturbing news. A rebellion had erupted among the Veneti tribe along the coast of northwestern Gaul. The Veneti were fishermen and sailors. Caesar sent immediate orders that ships should be built on the Loire River. Thousands of Roman soldiers and Gallic slaves spent all of spring hammering together a fleet. All was nearly ready when Caesar arrived.

A GREAT SEA BATTLE

"Of all the countries on the whole seacoast, the Veneti have by far the greatest influence," Caesar realized, "for they have many ships . . ."[1] The Romans were better soldiers than sailors. Roman ships moved slowly through the water. They greatly depended upon galley slaves to row them forward. The ships of the Veneti, however, were designed to move swiftly in shallow coastal waters.

Through most of the summer, Caesar's fleet attacked Veneti strongholds along the Quiberon coast. Whenever he captured a town or fort, the Veneti escaped by boat. Caesar soon understood that in order to beat these Gauls he must defeat them in a major sea battle. He began to make his plans. He cleverly ordered that sharp-pointed hooks be attached to long poles. These hooked poles were given to all of the Roman ships. Then the fleet sailed out to do battle.

The clash of Caesar's fleet against the Veneti was the first recorded naval battle in the Atlantic Ocean. During the sea battle, the Romans sailed up close beside the enemy ships. The Roman sailors then used their hooked poles. They hooked the ropes that attached the Veneti sails to their masts. Then the Roman galley slaves rowed hard ahead until the ropes were cut and the Veneti sails crashed down. Unable to sail away, the Veneti ships were at the mercy of the Roman ships. Luckily for Caesar, in the midst of the battle the wind also died. Roman soldiers boarded and captured one defenseless Veneti ship after another. From a cliff on the coast, Caesar watched as the entire enemy fleet was destroyed.

The naval battle became a tremendous victory for Caesar. The Veneti humbly surrendered. Caesar coldly ordered all of the Veneti leaders executed. The rest of the tribe he sold into slavery. His ruthless punishment of the Veneti had a purpose. It showed Gaul's other tribes what they could expect if they revolted.

A Massacre of German Tribes

After defeating the Veneti, Caesar turned his attention to the northern coast of Gaul. He marched his army into the territory of the rebellious Moroni tribe. This was the region between the Straits of Dover and the mouth of the Rhine River. The Roman troops burned many Moroni villages and farms. As 56 B.C. came to a close, Caesar's army went into winter camps in the valley of the lower Seine River. It would not be long before they were on the march again.

Early in 55 B.C., two Germanic tribes, the Usipetes and the Tencteri, crossed the Rhine River. They pushed southward, raiding the present-day Ardennes region of Belgium. Although fierce, the German warriors hoped to remain at peace with the Romans. The leaders of the German tribes came to Caesar's camp to discuss the situation. Caesar happily made them all his prisoners. This was against the honorable rules of war. But Caesar did not care. He felt sure the leaderless German raiders could now be easily defeated. He formed his army for battle and quickly marched it eight miles to the German camp. The enemy hardly realized the Romans were upon them. Caesar reported, "Those who could speedily take up arms resisted our men for a while, and fought amidst the carts and baggage [wagons]; but the rest of the crowd, consisting of women and children . . . began to flee in all directions."[2] Caesar sent squadrons of cavalry chasing after them.

The Roman horsemen chased the fleeing Germans to the banks of the Meuse and the Rhine rivers. They stabbed at the helpless enemy with their spears. Thousands of Germans threw themselves into the water and drowned while trying to swim to safety. Both the Usipetes and Tencteri tribes were destroyed. Caesar finally released the tribe leaders who were his prisoners and sent them away.

CROSSING THE RHINE

Having defeated these German raiders, Caesar decided to cross the Rhine River. He wished to prevent future German crossings into Gaul. By crossing the river, he would show the Germans the power of his army in their own homeland.

Near present-day Coblenz, Germany, Caesar ordered a bridge built. The river was about four hundred yards wide and twenty-five feet deep at that point. Roman officers and men set to work. Axemen chopped down trees. Sweating blacksmiths hammered iron into nails over hot fires. On boats, soldiers lay logs in the water and tied them into place. The construction progressed quickly. "The whole work," Caesar revealed, "was completed within ten days after the timber had begun to be collected . . ."[3]

It was a Roman engineering marvel. The Germans of the region were truly astonished that such a thing could be done and so fast. They retreated into the forests, as the Romans marched across the Rhine. The Roman invaders stayed in the area long enough to burn "all their villages and buildings [and] cut down the standing grain . . ." remarked Caesar.[4] The raid into Germany lasted eighteen days. Then Caesar ordered his soldiers back across the river. He had the bridge destroyed so the Germans could not use it.

INTO BRITAIN

News of Caesar's raid into Germany greatly excited citizens in Rome. In the late summer of 55 B.C., Caesar also decided to land soldiers on the island of Britain. No Roman army had ever landed on Britain. The great island north of Gaul was still a mystery to the Roman world. It was guessed that Britain held huge riches in gold, silver, iron, and tin. Caesar wanted to learn more about the land and its people. A raid into Britain would, of course, bring him greater fame as well.

When plans were completed, Caesar sailed with two legions in eighty transport ships and warships. Eighteen other ships were expected to follow with cavalry aboard. Caesar crossed the English Channel at the point where it was narrowest. The ships soon approached the high chalky cliffs near present-day Dover, England. Ranged along the cliffs stood thousands of British warriors. Caesar realized it would be difficult to make a landing here. He ordered his fleet to follow the coast farther to the northeast.

Britain was a difficult region to invade because it was an island. The invasion was a true test of the Roman Army and Navy.

Several miles up the coast, Caesar ordered a landing on the beach. The British tribesmen had followed the fleet up the coast. As the Roman transport ships reached the sandy shore, an army of screaming Britons charged down upon them. "The natives . . . sent forward their cavalry and chariot-fighters," wrote Caesar.[5] In battle, British warriors painted their faces blue. It gave them a wild and frightening appearance.

Caesar separated his warships from the transports. He ordered them to run ashore farther up the beach. The warships soon reached a flanking position. Roman archers aboard the ships sent arrows whistling through the air. Slingers swung and released small stones from leather pouches, sending them like a deadly hailstorm down on enemy heads. Catapults aboard the warships hurled large rocks upon the Britons. "The natives, frightened by the shape of our ships, the motion of the oars, and the strange type of artillery, halted and retreated just a little," commented Caesar.[6]

From the transport ships, the Roman soldiers were trying to land. But they were still under attack. The water came up to their chests, and they were wearing their heavy packs. One brave soldier in each legion carried its standard. This was a long wooden pole with a carved eagle at the top and the legion's painted number. The standard bearer of the Xth Legion decided to inspire his fellow Romans. "Leap down, fellow soldiers," he cried out, "unless you wish to betray your eagle to the enemy; I, at any rate, shall do my duty to my country and my general."[7] He then jumped into the waves and led the way ashore.

The landing of Caesar's army proved a most brave and thrilling feat. There was heavy fighting on the beach, but the Britons finally retreated. Afterward, the leaders of some of the British tribes met with Caesar and agreed to peace. Caesar soon realized he could not safely march his troops inland. The Roman cavalry never did arrive. Their ships were forced by a sudden storm to return to Gaul. Without cavalry, Caesar could not pursue the enemy with any speed. At the same time, the storm damaged many of the ships Caesar did have. His army was stranded on the British coast. In this emergency, Caesar immediately set his troops to work. They patched their damaged ships as well as they could. After a raid of only eighteen days, the Roman army sailed back to Gaul.

Caesar had not conquered Britain. He had hardly explored the island. Still, no other Roman had ever landed there before. In Rome, news of his adventure set tongues wagging and heads nodding in wonder. The Senate voted Caesar a thanksgiving honor even greater than before, a celebration of twenty days.

A Second Invasion

The spring of 54 B.C. found Caesar preparing his soldiers for a more serious invasion of Britain. During the winter, the Roman troops hammered together a new fleet of ships. Caesar designed these ships himself. They were lower, wider, and easier to steer. He planned to take to Britain five of the eight legions with him in Gaul. Two thousand Gallic horsemen also agreed to go. Altogether, Caesar's invasion army would number as many as thirty thousand men.

Near the end of July, Caesar began his grand adventure. Six hundred transports and warships set out with the Roman army. Another two hundred Roman merchant ships followed. The entire fleet landed on the coast of present-day Kent, England. The very sight of so many enemy ships sent the British fleeing inland. The Romans landed without a fight. They began marching in pursuit of the blue-faced British warriors. The armies clashed in several skirmishes. But then the British always raced away in their chariots.

At last, the Roman troops reached as far as England's present-day Hertford region. They stood on the southern bank of the Thames River. Beyond was the territory of the British king Cassivellaunus. From across the broad river, British warriors shouted insults. Caesar was determined to cross the river and fight. He ordered his troops forward. "Though they were in water up to the chin," Caesar exclaimed, "the soldiers advanced with such speed and such spirit that the enemy could not withstand the attack . . . but left the banks and took to flight."[8]

Once on the north bank of the Thames River, the Romans marched as far north as present-day Wheathampstead. The Romans could not force the British to fight a full-scale battle. But they destroyed many towns and farms. "Cassivellaunus . . . had [suffered] many losses, and . . . his territory had been laid waste . . ." commented Caesar.[9] Finally, the British king asked for a peace treaty.

Caesar had scored another amazing success. He had explored Britain and had made it possible for Roman traders to do business there. He realized he could not keep his army supplied. To remain in Britain would be unwise. After two months, he ended his invasion. At the end of September, the Roman army returned to Gaul.

A Great Loss

Caesar reached the shores of Gaul in the fall of 54 B.C. As he left his command ship, he was handed letters from Rome. Sadly, he learned that his twenty-two-year-old daughter, Julia, Pompey's wife, had died while giving birth. The baby boy lived only a few days longer than his mother. For the next three days, Caesar remained inside his army tent. Heartbroken, he mourned the loss of his only child. But as the Roman historian Seneca tells us, at last he "returned to his duties and conquered grief as quickly as he was [used] to conquer everything."[10]

The death of his daughter affected Caesar personally and politically. The marriage bond that had united Caesar and Pompey no longer existed. By this time, Crassus and Pompey both had become governors of their own provinces. Crassus was in Syria making plans to invade the neighboring kingdom of Parthia. Pompey had become governor of all of Spain. While Pompey remained in Italy, he let trusted officers perform his duties in Spain.

UNREST IN GAUL

All was not peaceful in Gaul in the fall of 54 B.C. Caesar recorded that some of Gaul's bravest tribes "could not bear to submit to Roman rule."[11] The trouble started among the Carnutes who lived around Cenabum (present-day Orleans). Led by Ambiorix, the king of the Eburones, they rose up in rebellion. They first attacked the Roman fort at Aduatuca (north of present-day Liege, Belgium). One and a half Roman legions were completely massacred.

When he learned of the disaster, Caesar allowed his hair and beard to grow. He insisted he would not cut them until he got revenge. In his province of Cisalpine Gaul, Caesar enlisted two new legions. Pompey loaned him another legion of his own. Word soon reached Caesar of further unrest. The Eburones, along with warriors of the Nervii, the Atuatuci, and other tribes, had surrounded a Roman fort in the territory of the Nervii. It stood in the present-day province of Hainaut in Belgium. A single Roman legion, commanded by Quintus Cicero (brother of Marcus Tullius Cicero), was surrounded and under attack by sixty thousand Gauls.

Caesar made a hurried march northward. He must save the Roman fort. He kept his soldiers on the road twenty-five miles a day. As Caesar neared the fort, the enemy marched out to confront him. Caesar quickly devised a plan to trick them. He built a small walled camp. It made his army appear smaller than it really was. Inside the camp, Caesar ordered that "the men should rush about as much as possible."[12] He had them behave as if they were afraid. He also ordered his cavalry to retreat, as though scared of the Gauls.

The Gauls rushed uphill toward the camp, expecting an easy victory. In an instant, Caesar ordered the blare of trumpets. Thousands of Roman soldiers suddenly poured out of the camp gates. The Gauls were stunned by the sight. "Not one man stood his ground to fight," claimed Caesar afterwards.[13] The Gauls instead fled in all directions. The army of Ambiorix ceased to exist. Caesar had saved General Cicero and his besieged garrison.

FURTHER FIGHTING

Ambiorix had been defeated, but other rebellious Gauls remained. Caesar immediately marched four legions against the Nervii. Then with five legions he hurried into present-day Holland to battle the Menapii. He forced both tribes to beg for peace. At the same time, he sent one of his best generals, Labienus, to fight the Treveri tribe. The Roman army fought bravely and defeated the Treveri.

When Caesar rejoined Labienus, they marched together to the Rhine River. Caesar ordered a second bridge built and rushed his troops across it. He wished to throw a scare into the Germans. He wanted to prevent them from sending warriors across the water to help the Gauls fight Rome. The raid into Germany was brief, but it succeeded in its purpose.

As the weather turned cold, Caesar spent the last of the year putting down revolts among Gaul's Belgian tribes. His combined army of ten legions had become the largest military force in all of the Roman world. Caesar did not travel to Cisalpine Gaul that winter as usual. To crush the spirit of rebellion in Gaul, he remained with his army.

THE DEATH OF CRASSUS

By 53 B.C., sixty-year-old Crassus, governor of Syria, had gathered a Roman army of more than forty thousand soldiers. At last, he felt ready to invade Parthia (present-day Iraq and northern Syria). He hoped to win military glory equal to Caesar's and Pompey's. Things did not go as he planned. In June, at Carrhae in the Syrian desert, Crassus found himself surrounded by Parthian cavalry. Parthian archers fired so many arrows so quickly that the Romans were overwhelmed. More than thirty thousand

Roman soldiers died. Only ten thousand beaten men managed to escape the desert safely.

Crassus himself was killed in the battle. Victorious Parthians presented his cut-off head to their king. With the death of Crassus, Caesar had lost his greatest ally. Truly the Triumvirate was at an end. Now, only Caesar and Pompey remained.

CLODIUS VERSUS MILO

It was at this time that Caesar also learned of continued rioting in Rome. Near the end of 53 B.C., both Clodius and Milo were candidates for government offices. The fighting between their forces became worse than ever. Finally, on January 18, 52 B.C., Clodius was riding on the Appian Way just outside of Rome. Thirty of his men rode with him. On the road, they happened to meet Milo traveling in a coach with his wife Fausta. The coach was followed by about three hundred of Milo's personal guards. A fight broke out, and one of Milo's men thrust a spear. It pierced Clodius in the shoulder. Clodius' slaves carried their bleeding master into a nearby inn. Milo seized upon this chance to be rid of his enemy once and for all. He ordered his men into the inn. They first murdered the protesting innkeeper. Then they dragged Clodius out onto the cobblestone highway. There, they stabbed him repeatedly and left his body in the road. A passing senator later discovered the corpse and had it brought to Rome.

The next morning, January 19, a crowd led by Clodius' upset followers carried the body into the

75

Senate-House. They piled up whatever wood they could find to make a funeral pyre. It was the custom of Romans to burn their dead and bury the bones and ashes. The wild mob grabbed benches and tables for their fire. They filled their arms with scrolls from nearby bookstalls. Soon the flames were licking the ceiling beams of the Senate-House. The entire building then burned to the ground.

During the following days, the gangs of Clodius and Milo continued their violent street fights. Bloodshed threatened the safety of the entire city. Somehow the Senate needed to restore order. At the end of January, with the Senate-House destroyed, the Senate met in a theatre recently built by Pompey. Many senators agreed that Pompey was the only man with the power to save the Republic. Pompey accepted appointment as temporary consul. For the first time since the days of Sulla, armed troops were marched into Rome. Within weeks, Pompey had restored peace in the city.

Later in the year, Pompey married Cornelia. She was the daughter of one of Caesar's political enemies, Metellus Scipio. Pompey quickly arranged an election so that his new father-in-law could serve with him as co-consul for the rest of 52 B.C. News of these happenings, of course, reached Caesar in Gaul. He understood that a political gap was widening between him and Pompey.

THE
CONQUEST
OF GAUL

Word of the political unrest in Rome gave hope to many Gauls. In the spring of 52 B.C., the Carnute tribe rose up and attacked the town of Cenabum. The massacre of the Roman trading community in Cenabum sparked the beginning of another great revolt. The spirit of rebellion soon gripped half of Gaul. When the Arverni tribe learned of the massacre, they elected a young nobleman named Vercingetorix as their new king. Vercingetorix was a remarkable young man of about thirty years. He stood tall and impressive, with handsome features and a military bearing. It was said his name meant "King of Heroes."[1]

VERCINGETORIX
It was Vercingetorix who swiftly gathered together the Senones, Parisii, Pictones, Cadurci, Turoni, Aulerci,

Lemovices, Andes, and other tribes. Their leaders gave him overall command. Caesar himself tells us that Vercingetorix "urged them to take up arms for their common liberty."[2] Within days, Vercingetorix had put together a Gallic army of ten legions near Agedincum (about sixty miles southeast of present-day Paris).

From his winter headquarters in Cisalpine Gaul, Caesar realized he faced a great emergency. He immediately started northward. The soldiers traveling with him had to clear the way through six feet of snow. Caesar quickly reached his assembling legions at the Belgian frontier. Without rest, Caesar and his soldiers overwhelmed several rebel strongholds and captured Cenabum. He burned the town to ashes. After that, he faced Vercingetorix for the first time. At Noviodunum, south of Cenabum, Caesar sent allied German cavalry into battle. They beat Vercingetorix and forced him to retreat.

 AVARICUM

Caesar turned his attention toward the fortress town of Avaricum (present-day Bourges, France). If he could conquer it, he could bring the defending Bituriges tribe back under Roman control. Caesar walked among his busy soldiers as they constructed siege works outside the town. "In twenty-five days they built a ramp three hundred and thirty feet wide and eighty feet high," he later declared.[3]

The Gauls defending the town set fire to the siege towers. They tunneled beneath the dirt ramp, hoping it would collapse. But in the end the Romans still were able to conquer the town. Frustrated by the war, the Roman troops slaughtered everyone they could find. "Enraged by the massacre at Cenabum . . ." Caesar offered as an excuse, "the soldiers spared neither the aged, nor the women, nor the children."[4]

DEFEAT AT GERGOVIA

Vercingetorix had retreated to the Arverni fortress capital, Gergovia. It stood on a mountaintop near present-day Clermont-Ferrand, France. Caesar made his plans to capture Gergovia. At first, the Romans besieged the town. Then Caesar tried a surprise raid to break into it. "Both sides fought very fiercely at close quarters. . . ." exclaimed Caesar.[5] In the excitement, Caesar's troops disobeyed his orders. Having broken through the gates, the Romans tried to advance their attack far into the town. The Gauls made a violent counterattack. Caesar watched his stunned men streaming back down the hillside. More than seven hundred Roman soldiers were killed. It was a rare defeat for Caesar. He withdrew his bloodied army temporarily into the territory of the Aedui.

Word of the Roman failure at Gergovia spread fast. Additional tribes of Gauls now joined Vercingetorix's army. Even Aedui warriors entered Vercingetorix's camp to fight against the Romans. Vercingetorix declared, "The hour of victory has come."[6] The Gauls advanced on Caesar's army and attacked. By this time, Caesar had enlisted a large number of German cavalry. He formed his legions into a square. The cavalry of Vercingetorix could not break it up. In an unexpected counterattack,

Caesar's German cavalry overwhelmed the Gauls. Vercingetorix ordered a retreat. The Gauls took refuge in the mountain fortress of Alesia (present-day Alise-Sainte-Reine).

A DOUBLE BARRICADE AT ALESIA

"The town of Alesia was situated on top of a very high hill . . ." explained Caesar.[7] In fact, it stood on a plateau more than fifteen hundred feet high. Caesar wished to besiege Alesia, but he understood he would have to make careful plans. It is thought Caesar had an army of more than fifty thousand men. Vercingetorix possessed about an equal number inside the town.[8] At the same time, the Veneti, Nervii, Helvetii, Morini, Parisii, and other tribes began gathering at Bibracte, southwest of Alesia. They prepared to send a huge army to rescue Vercingetorix. Caesar realized he would have enemies both in front of him and behind him. He put his troops to work building an awesome double barricade.

Sweating soldiers cut down trees and raised twelve-foot wooden walls to encircle Alesia. The inside wall stretched ten miles. The outside wall was even longer, thirteen miles. Between the two barricades, Caesar ordered camps and forts built for his men. Caesar's troops scoured the countryside. They gathered enough grain to feed his ten legions for a month. Then they settled themselves within the safety of their double barricade and waited.

THE GAULS ATTACK

Inside Alesia, food began to grow scarce. Vercingetorix decided he must send away everyone who could not fight. A great line of old people, sick people, women, and children straggled out of Alesia's gates. They came to the inner Roman barricade and begged to be taken prisoner. Caesar refused to accept them. He forced them to return to Alesia. Vercingetorix would not let them back inside. So they camped outside the gates, sick and starving.

Shortly afterwards, the huge Gallic relief force arrived from Bibracte. They quickly prepared to attack Caesar's outer barricade. On the walls, the Romans gazed out upon an astonishing army of Gallic warriors and horsemen. The very next day, the Gauls charged the outer wall. Vercingetorix added to the pressure on Caesar's army. He made a rush from Alesia with his men.

The Romans fought off the heavy attacks. Shouts went up from all sides. Both Roman and Gallic soldiers displayed uncommon bravery. "Fighting had been going on," exclaimed Caesar, "with victory in doubt, from midday to almost sunset."[9] At last, Caesar's German cavalrymen were able to break up the attack of the Gallic relief force. The enemy fell back.

The next day, all remained quiet until midnight. Then, the Gauls attacked a second time from both sides. From a high observation point within his double barricade, Caesar scanned the battlefield. He hurriedly sent reinforcements wherever they were needed most. The Gauls fought with great courage. At times, the Romans were nearly overcome. Caesar rushed from place to place, urging his men to continue the fight. "Our men dropped their javelins and fought with their swords," he exclaimed.[10]

Again, Caesar's cavalry saved the battle. The horsemen suddenly attacked the Gauls from the rear. Caesar threw fresh soldiers into the fight. The Gallic relief force suffered panic and terrific slaughter. Caesar's cavalry captured seventy-four of the enemy's standards. These treasured legion emblems were brought to Caesar. Vercingetorix saw the relief force falling back. He unhappily called off his own attack and withdrew back into Alesia.

ROMAN VICTORY

The warriors of the Gallic relief force bandaged their wounded and prepared for a third attack. They had discovered that to the north the outer barricade had a weak point. The next day at noon, thousands of Gauls attacked that place, while Vercingetorix again charged the inner barricade from the Alesia side.

Dressed in his red commander's cloak, Caesar let himself be seen among his men. He shouted words of courage and hope. He shifted troops from his strong points to his weak ones. As the attacks continued, he quickly reorganized his tired men and sent them back into the battle. Finally, he personally led his last fresh troops directly into the fighting. Again his cavalry attacked the enemy's rear exactly when needed most. The Gauls in the relieving army were gripped with sudden fear. Caesar's grim horsemen galloped down among them as they broke and ran.

The Gauls had tried three times to break through Caesar's lines. Each time, they had failed. The next morning, the Gauls inside Alesia finally admitted their defeat. "Those who were in Alesia, having given themselves and Caesar much trouble, surrendered at last . . ." recorded the historian Plutarch.[11] Caesar ordered that the Gallic warriors throw their weapons in a pile. He demanded that their leaders present themselves to him. The Gauls humbly came forth from Alesia and did as they were instructed. Plutarch later described the arrival of Vercingetorix. The defeated Gallic king "leaped down from his horse, stripped off his armor, and sat at Caesar's feet silent and motionless until he was led away under arrest . . ."[12]

In the end, Caesar decided to grant pardons to all of the warriors of the Aedui and Arverni tribes. They had been Roman allies before. He needed friends now to strengthen his influence in Gaul. However, the rest of his prisoners he enslaved. He made gifts of one Gaul to each of his soldiers. The rest he most likely sold to Roman slave dealers and kept the profit himself.[13] Caesar's victory at Alesia was perhaps his greatest military achievement. Although hugely outnumbered, he had defeated two enemy armies at the same time.

CAESAR THE WRITER

The capture of Alesia brought an end to most of the rebellion in Gaul. Caesar established his winter headquarters at Bibracte. At the end of 52 B.C., he finished writing a history. In *The Gallic War*, he personally told the story of his conquest of Gaul.

The Gallic War is divided into eight short books, one for each year of Caesar's military campaigns in Germany, Britain, and Gaul. *The Gallic War* has been used in classrooms for centuries. Even Cicero greatly admired Caesar's writing style and his descriptions in *The Gallic War*: "They are . . . straight and beautiful . . . clear and correct," he wrote.[14]

Caesar's writings suggest that he believed he and his army were on a mission. The Romans wished to spread Roman law and order throughout the world. They wanted to bring Roman trade and culture to people they considered barbarians.

It also seems Caesar desired to advertise himself and his accomplishments. Roman readers in his day could not fail to be impressed with all he described. Perhaps Caesar sometimes exaggerated the numbers and strength of his enemies. Nonetheless, *The Gallic War* is still fascinating to read.

CAESAR THE GENERAL

With the conquest of Gaul, forty-seven-year-old Julius Caesar had proven himself a great general. Cicero called him "terribly active, swift and prudent."[15] There is no question that he was a bold and brilliant leader of his troops. He had the rare ability to excite in them fierce pride and loyalty. One officer declared that the soldiers loved his "wonderful good spirits."[16]

ROMAN BOOKS

Roman books were not printed on presses and bound between stiff covers like books today. Instead, each book was copied by hand on long rolls of paper made from the papyrus plant. Some rolls were thirty feet long. The job of copying books was often done by educated slaves. In Roman writing there was no difference between capital letters and lowercase letters. Words had no spaces between them. Sentences had no punctuation. There were no paragraphs to separate ideas. Reading a Roman book was a challenge.

Caesar molded his men into excellent soldiers by personal example, both in camp and in battle. The writer Plutarch remarked, "There was no danger to which he did not willingly expose himself."[17] Caesar's soldiers were astonished to see a general willing to suffer the same hardships they did. The Roman biographer Suetonius recorded that Caesar "handled weapons with great skill, was an excellent rider, and had amazing [energy]. On marches he sometimes led on horseback, but more often on foot, bare-headed [without a helmet] . . ."[18]

Caesar was not only a fine example to the common soldier. He won the respect of his officers, too. Time and time again, he proved himself highly skilled in army organization and planning. He was quick, inventive, and always ready to learn new tactics and strategy. He also knew how to communicate his ideas. One officer, Hirtius, remarked, "Caesar possessed . . . the surest skill in explaining his own plans."[19] Finally, Caesar was willing to take chances. Repeatedly, he calculated his risks, and in the end his gambles were successful.

KEEPING THE PEACE

Near the end of 52 B.C., the Senate honored Caesar by ordering a twenty-day thanksgiving celebration in Rome. In eight years, Caesar had won an incredible two hundred thousand square miles of territory for Rome. Caesar knew his time as governor would soon end. He wished to prevent any more outbreaks of fighting in Gaul. His officer Hirtius later wrote, "He therefore showed the tribes every possible honor . . ."[20] He rewarded loyal Gallic leaders and kept taxes low. He only demanded that the Gauls pay Rome a yearly tribute of 40 million sesterces. Sulla, when he conquered Asia, had demanded 480 million sesterces a year from that province.

Caesar demanded that the Gauls surrender some land for Roman colonists. But he let them keep most of their property and allowed them to rule under their own laws and customs. It seemed peace had come to Gaul at last. But Caesar sensed new dangers brewing in Rome. The consul Marcus Marcellus insisted that if the Gallic war had truly ended then Caesar's legions should be sent home.[21] Caesar guessed the Senate wished to take his power from him. There were Romans who regarded Caesar as a threat to the Republic. In the fall of 50 B.C., he camped his legions in winter quarters in Gaul. He then set off across the Alps to Cisalpine Gaul and established his own headquarters at Ravenna.

■

CIVIL WAR

Caesar's second term as governor had neared its end. During his career as a general, his armies had fought more than thirty major battles. According to the writer Plutarch, Caesar and his soldiers had captured over eight hundred towns and killed more than one million people.[1] The Roman Senate found it hard to find fault with the conqueror of Gaul. Yet many senators feared his return to Rome. The idea of Caesar being elected consul again made them very nervous. Caesar's political enemies believed that as consul, with his loyal soldiers to support him, Caesar meant to ruin the Republic.

It was true the Triumvirate had fallen apart. Pompey now held the same view as most of the Senate. He regarded Caesar as a giant threat to his own power and influence. Plutarch later recorded the belief that "Caesar had long ago decided that he must get rid of Pompey— just as Pompey, of course, had decided to get rid of Caesar . . ."[2] In Gaul, Caesar had trained a huge army and reached the height of military success. His career as a general now challenged the pride of the great Pompey.

A PLAN TO WEAKEN CAESAR

On December 1, 50 B.C., the Senate decided that a new governor should be sent north to replace Caesar. One of

Caesar's supporters, the tribune Gaius Scribonius Curio, used his veto to prevent the order from going into effect. Caesar instructed Curio to tell the Senate that both he and Pompey should resign their military commands. It would keep their power equal. By a vote of 370–22, the senators approved this plan. Here was an opportunity to remove both Caesar and Pompey as threats. The few senators who were Caesar's greatest enemies, however, found a tribune who vetoed the plan.

The next day, Consul Marcellus and several senators made a visit to Pompey, who was living just outside the city. They asked that Pompey protect Rome and save the Republic. They feared that Caesar might march on the city. Pompey hesitated, but he did not turn down the request.

On December 10, new tribunes were elected. One of them was Marc Antony (Marcus Antonius). Marc Antony had been one of Caesar's most loyal army officers in Gaul. He was a tall, handsome man. The writer Plutarch later declared that, "his well-shaped beard, wide forehead and curved nose gave him a manly appearance . . ."[3] In character, Marc Antony was a pleasure-seeker. He enjoyed going to the theatre, drinking, dining, and pursuing women.

In the new session of the Senate, Pompey's son-in-law Scipio rose to speak. He offered a motion demanding that Caesar give up his armies or be thought of as a traitor. Marc Antony angrily spoke out against the motion. Marc Antony had a letter from Caesar read in the Senate. In it, Caesar offered again to surrender his command if Pompey did the same. The Senate responded with a declaration. Caesar would be considered a public enemy if he did not give up his legions within two months. It seemed the Senate preferred to put their trust in Pompey rather than in Caesar. On January 7, Marc Antony and a fellow tribune, Quintus Cassius, hurried north to report to Julius Caesar in Cisalpine Gaul.

THE GREAT DECISION

Caesar was faced with a most serious choice. He could surrender his army and submit to the will of the Senate. This would be an insult to his sense of dignity. It would ruin his political career and might even endanger his life. He did not wish to be brought to trial for things he had done as consul in 59 B.C. On the other hand, Caesar could defy the Senate. By keeping his army, he could keep his power. But it would mean civil war.

Caesar had only the XIIIth Legion with him in Cisalpine Gaul. He ordered it, as well as some Gallic and German cavalry, across the Rubicon River into Italy. On the day of January 9, 49 B.C., Caesar attended a play, went over designs for building a gladiator school, and dined at a banquet. He had told no one what his final response to the Senate would be. "Then, after sunset," described biographer Suetonius, "he took mules from a nearby bakery, harnessed them to a carriage, and set out very secretly with a small escort."[4] On his nighttime journey, his lamps went out. He and his men got lost in the dark. Near dawn, he found a guide who led the group forward by narrow trails. At last, they reached the Rubicon River. It marked the boundary into Roman

Italy. To cross the Rubicon, Caesar knew, would be a declaration of war.

At the river's edge, he wrestled with his conscience. Finally, he exclaimed, "The die is cast." He had made his decision. Caesar led his officers across the river.

ON THE MARCH

On the morning of January 12, 49 B.C., the XIIIth Legion, along with the Gallic and German cavalry, assembled in the town square at Ariminum (Rimini, Italy). Caesar, wearing his red commander's cloak, stepped before them. In a speech, Caesar described how his enemies in the Senate had wronged him. "I have been your commander for nine years," he declared. "Under my leadership your efforts on Rome's behalf have been crowned with good fortune. . . . Now I ask you to defend my reputation and standing against the assaults of my enemies."[5] He pulled open his tunic and showed his bare chest. He was willing to die by the sword, if his men would follow him. He promised great rewards, as well as danger. But he insisted his cause was just and honorable. His soldiers loudly cheered him when he finished. They vowed to give him their loyal support.

From Ariminum, Caesar sent part of his legion along the coast toward the town of Ancona. Another part marched across the Apennine Mountains toward Arretium (present-day Arezzo). Caesar himself started south with troops toward Picenum. By January 14, Ancona and Arretium had surrendered. During the next few days, other towns also opened their gates to Caesar's troops. Pesar, Fano, Gubbio, and Osimo all surrendered without a fight.

THE PARDON OF CORFINIUM

By the middle of February, Caesar welcomed more of his legions from Gaul. He and his army camped outside the walled city of Corfinium. It was at Corfinium, east of Rome, that Caesar faced his first serious resistance. Inside the city were eighteen thousand soldiers commanded by Domitius Ahenobarbus. Ahenobarbus surely wished to fight. The arrival of Caesar's reinforcements, however, robbed the republican troops of their fighting spirit.

The defense of Corfinium collapsed within days. As they surrendered, Caesar unexpectedly let them all go free. He had decided to pardon them. Caesar had chosen to make it his policy to show great mercy to his enemies in this war. On February 20, 49 B.C., Caesar enlisted Ahenobarbus' soldiers into his own army.

Word of Caesar's "Pardon of Corfinium" spread swiftly. Many old enemies, however, found Caesar's mercy insulting. Caesar's kindness to them was shameful to republican Romans who treasured their honor.

POMPEY'S RETREAT

Caesar's rapid march into Italy shocked many Romans. At the head of his troops, he took control of Picenum with surprising speed. Picenum was Pompey's home territory. Plutarch later recorded that when news of

Caesar's Rubicon crossing "came flying to Rome . . . the city was filled with . . . a fear that was beyond compare."[6] Pompey had been asked to defend Rome and the Republic. On January 17, however, Pompey decided to abandon the city. Many senators and government officials fled the city that night. They fled in such a panic that they left the contents of the Treasury behind. Pompey had once boasted, "I only have to stamp my foot, and all over Italy legionaries and cavalry will rise up from the ground."[7] Now that he needed them, however, he found it difficult to raise troops in Italy.

Caesar reached Brindisi on the southeast coast of Italy in the middle of March. He was too late and had too few troops to prevent Pompey from escaping the city by ship. Pompey sailed across the Adriatic Sea to Greece. He took command of the growing republican army there. It was just sixty-five days since Caesar had crossed the Rubicon. He had conquered all of Italy with amazing ease. He also controlled the provinces of Cisalpine Gaul, Transalpine Gaul, Illyricum, and Gaul. For the moment, he gave up the idea of chasing after Pompey. Instead, he decided to send troops to occupy the island provinces of Sardinia and Sicily. He himself planned to march into Spain.

A Brief Stop in Rome

Caesar sent out messengers calling upon the Senate to assemble in Rome on April 1, 49 B.C. He himself arrived on that day, almost exactly nine years after he first left for Gaul. Only a few senators met him at the city gates.

Caesar made them an offer and a threat. "I earnestly invite you to join with me in carrying on the government of Rome," he told them.[8] But he also warned that if they refused he would govern without them.

After entering Rome, Caesar's troops broke into the government treasury at the Temple of Saturn. Inside, they discovered fifteen thousand bars of gold, thirty thousand pieces of silver, and 30 million sesterce in coins. Here was the money Caesar needed to pay for his war. He gave Marc Antony command of all the troops in Italy. General Marcus Aemilius Lepidus was left to rule in Rome in Caesar's name. After just eight days in the city, Caesar himself set out for Spain. He took with him three legions and nine hundred armed horsemen.

AT WAR IN SPAIN

Just twelve days after leaving Rome, Caesar reached Massilia on the southern coast of Transalpine Gaul (present-day Marseille, France). The city leaders of Massilia announced they wanted to remain neutral. They refused to open the gates to him. In response, on June 5, Caesar ordered his troops to start siege operations. He left his general Trebonius in charge and continued on to Spain.

Already, he had ordered six legions from Gaul into Spain. By June 22, 49 B.C., he reached their camp. The soldiers greeted him with cheers. They were ready for action, and Caesar bragged they "could tear down the heavens themselves."[9] Caesar marched his army to Ilerda (present-day Lerida, Spain). Five legions loyal to

Pompey occupied this mountain fortress that overlooked the Segre River. The Pompeian army was commanded by Lucius Afranius and Marcus Petreius. Caesar faced difficulty in preparing his attack. Unexpected flooding destroyed the bridges over the river. In order to cross the river, Caesar ordered his soldiers to build light, sturdy boats. They were designed like ones he had seen in Britain. The soldiers carried the boats on wagons twenty-two miles upstream in the darkness of night. He ordered some of his soldiers to cross the river in the boats. Working from both sides of the river, the soldiers then swiftly completed a new bridge in two days.

Advancing downstream, Caesar stunned the enemy in a surprise attack. His troops hounded them as they retreated. The Pompeian army was at last surrounded and besieged. On August 27, they finally surrendered. Just as before, Caesar offered his enemies mercy. To General Afranius, he demanded, "I repeat, you are to disband your armies and leave the province: if my orders are obeyed no one shall suffer."[10] In just forty days, Caesar had destroyed Pompey's best army and taken Spain with hardly any fighting. By the end of September, he set out for Italy. On his return march, Massilia also finally surrendered.

ACROSS THE ADRIATIC SEA

In December 49 B.C., Caesar swept into Rome for a brief visit of eleven days. He had himself and a supporter, Publius Servilius Isauricus, elected consuls for 48 B.C. Then he turned his attention again to Pompey. By this time, Caesar controlled the western half of the Roman Empire: Gaul, Spain, Sardinia, Corsica, Sicily, and Italy. He had sent Curio into the province of Africa. But Curio had died in battle and lost his three legions to forces loyal to Pompey. Pompey's navy had also scored a victory over Caesar's warships in the Adriatic Sea between Italy and Greece.

Most dangerous of all to Caesar was Pompey himself. Pompey had brought five legions with him from Italy to Greece. Six more legions were marching to him from Asia and Syria. Pompey had spent months training his troops. He had organized a great fleet in the Adriatic and had gathered supplies to support his army.

At Brindisi, Italy, Caesar assembled twelve legions and more than a thousand cavalry. It was a strong army, but he lacked a strong navy. He only possessed enough transport ships to carry about twenty thousand soldiers and six hundred cavalrymen. On January 4, 48 B.C., Caesar crossed the Adriatic Sea with these men. He landed at Palissa in present-day Albania. Caesar had surprised Pompey with his first crossing. But now Pompey's great fleet was on guard and on patrol. Caesar would have great difficulty getting the rest of his army safely across the sea.

Caesar established a camp just north of the Greek town of Apollonia. Pompey hurried his army forward and established his camp on the opposite side of the Apsus River. With the armies encamped close to each other, Caesar decided to try peace talks with Pompey. He sent his officer Publius Vatinius to the riverbank to shout his offer across the water. Other soldiers soon flocked on both sides of the river. Old friends called back and forth. Suddenly, under orders, archers on Pompey's side of the water let loose their arrows. Some of Caesar's retreating soldiers fell wounded. This was the work of General Labienus. Once one of Caesar's best generals, Labienus had chosen to join Pompey's side in the civil war. "Now then," shouted Labienus across the river, "stop talking about an agreement. Until Caesar's head is delivered to us, there can be no peace."[11] There would be no friendly arrangement between Caesar and Pompey this time. From now on, there would be only deadly battle.

CAESAR AND FORTUNE

At Apollonia, Caesar impatiently waited for the rest of his army to arrive from Italy. Finally, he decided to cross the Adriatic Sea in a small boat, in order to make arrangements personally. It was a dangerous mission, so he traveled disguised as a slave. On the sea voyage, the boat sailed into a terrible storm. The boat captain announced that he wanted to turn back. Caesar shouted in his ear, "Go on, my friend, and fear nothing; you carry Caesar and his fortune in your boat."[12] The Romans believed greatly in fortune. Caesar himself had once admitted, "Fortune plays a large part in all affairs, and especially in warfare."[13] On this occasion, however, good fortune was not with Caesar. The howling wind and fearsome waves proved so strong that the little boat had to turn back.

CAESAR'S ARMY IN GREECE

On April 10, Marc Antony finally brought the rest of Caesar's army across the sea from Italy. Caesar now commanded an army of eleven legions. It was still smaller than Pompey's, but he could at last begin the fight. Caesar boldly planned to encircle Pompey's camp near the coastal town of Dyrrachium. He would construct a fifteen-mile siege line.

Caesar put his army into motion. In time, he managed to get it into position between Pompey's army and its supply base at Dyrrachium. Caesar's troops began cutting trees and erecting forts and barricades. "The traditional purpose of siege operations is to cut off your enemy from supplies," Caesar later declared. "Yet we were blockading a force of unbeaten soldiers, who outnumbered us and were short of nothing."[14]

In fact, it was Caesar's army that needed supplies. Some of Caesar's hungry men found a kind of local root called chara. The soldiers crushed and mixed the chara with milk. They made a kind of dough from it that they baked into bread. Troops in Pompey's lines sometimes shouted insults about the hunger that plagued Caesar's army. Caesar's soldiers answered these insults. They defiantly flung loaves of their chara bread over their walls toward the enemy. "The soldiers," Caesar proudly stated, ". . . were often heard saying that they would sooner live on the bark of trees than allow Pompey to escape."[15]

DEFEAT AT DYRRACHIUM

Caesar's legions had pinned Pompey's army against the seacoast by forming a large semicircle around it. After weeks of siege, in July 48 B.C., Pompey at last decided to make an attack. Thirty-six thousand of his men struck a weak point at the southern end of Caesar's siege line. Smoke signals sent from hill to hill warned Caesar. He hurried soldiers forward to defend the line. But several of Pompey's legions had already broken through. Caesar ordered his men to fall back and build new barricades close by.

It was clear Pompey planned to attack here again. Caesar quickly planned a move of his own. He secretly led some twenty thousand soldiers up to Pompey's camp. He then signaled the order to attack. Pompey's cavalry responded by striking Caesar's men as they were crossing over a narrow dam. It was a lucky stroke for Pompey. Caesar's troops panicked and turned back to escape. Some jumped from the dam into the water below and drowned. Others fell and were trampled to death. Caesar tried to stop his fleeing soldiers. He grabbed a legion standard and shouted orders to halt. But his men could not be stopped. The attack of Caesar's men was a complete failure.

Pompey was surprised by his own success. He worried that his troops might fall into an ambush. He had a chance to destroy Caesar once and for all, but he refused to press his advantage. Altogether, Caesar had lost 960 foot soldiers and two hundred cavalrymen.

In Pompey's camp, the Romans celebrated victory. Caesar, however, spent a very restless night. By morning, he had decided upon a new plan to beat Pompey. He assembled his army and urged the men not to lose their fighting spirit. He reminded them of their many successes in the past. He later wrote, "My earlier hopes had been disappointed, and it was evident that we needed an entirely new plan of campaign."[16] As a result, he ordered that the siege at Dyrrachium be abandoned.

THE PLAIN OF PHARSALUS

Caesar marched his army two hundred miles inland. He appeared to be retreating. But as Pompey's army followed, it was being drawn away from its supply base on the seacoast. At last, Caesar's dusty soldiers arrived at the village of Pharsalus. Their morale remained low as they watched Pompey's army arrive and camp on a nearby hill. It is believed Pompey's army numbered about fifty thousand soldiers while Caesar's force was about thirty thousand.[17] Pompey, however, seemed afraid to attack. As the days passed, Caesar's men grew more confident.

The Roman senators traveling with Pompey demanded that he fight. Finally, on August 9, 48 B.C., Caesar saw Pompey's army marching into battle formation. Caesar's troops had been about to continue their retreat. Now, however, Caesar excitedly ordered his red commander's cloak draped before his tent. This was his signal for a fight. "We shall have to postpone our journey and think of battle," Caesar called out to his soldiers. "That is what we have worked for all along. Let us meet the enemy with stout hearts: we shall not easily find another opportunity like this."[18]

INTO BATTLE

The armies of Pompey and Caesar both marched into battle formation. Two of Rome's greatest generals were about to fight one another. Caesar gestured for the trumpeters to blow the signal for attack. Just before the call for action, a veteran soldier named Crastinus stepped forward. He cried out, "Come on, my old comrades; do for Caesar as you have always done. This is our last fight; victory will restore to him his dignity and to us our freedom." He then shouted to Caesar, "Sir, I will make you proud of me to-day, alive or dead."[19]

Caesar placed his Roman legions in the center of his battle line. Cavalry squadrons of Gauls and Germans took positions on the left and right flanks. Hundreds of archers and slingers stood among the troops. To the right, Caesar stood among the soldiers of the Xth Legion. On low ground behind that part of the battle line, he had hidden three thousand of his best troops. He had given them special instructions. When the enemy cavalry attacked they were to jump up and thrust their spears at their heads. Caesar believed these young enemy cavalrymen who had no battle experience would fear any injury to their faces.

The sound of both Pompey's and Caesar's trumpeters pierced the ears of thousands of soldiers. Officers hurried among the troops on both sides, urging courage. The two armies started for each other across the open plain. At the proper distance, Caesar ordered his troops to throw their javelins and draw their swords.

As Caesar had guessed, Pompey's cavalry began to get in behind the Xth Legion. Caesar waited for the perfect moment. Then he signaled to his hidden spearmen. They jumped up and thrust their spears in the faces of the enemy horsemen. Just as Caesar had guessed, the cavalrymen turned their horses in sudden and confused retreat. On the right flank, the threat of cavalry to Caesar's men was gone. The troops there pressed forward and began to encircle Pompey's foot soldiers. They swiftly outflanked the infantry and began striking them down with their swords.

Pompey's archers and slingers began to weaken and fall back in fear. Many of them fell killed. Caesar ordered fresh troops into the fight. Fearing total destruction, all along Pompey's line soldiers began to throw down their weapons and run. By noontime, even Pompey knew he had lost the battle.

The old soldier Crastinus had kept his promise to Caesar. In the battle, he had fought like a hero. Plutarch later revealed, "At last he was struck . . . by the wound of a sword, which went in at his mouth with such force that it came out at his neck behind."[20]

The Cost of Victory

Pompey had put too much faith in his cavalrymen. They had fled the battlefield. Caesar's soldiers charged ahead all the way into Pompey's camp. According to the writer

Plutarch, Pompey exclaimed in shock, "What, into the camp too?"[21] He mounted a horse and galloped away, barely escaping capture. That evening, Caesar dined in Pompey's command tent. He and his officers enjoyed the victory dinner that had been prepared by Pompey's camp cooks.

Later, Caesar walked upon the battlefield. The dead lay motionless. The wounded moaned and cried out for water. The historian Suetonius later noted that Caesar gazed at the horrors around him and grimly stated, "This was their own doing."[22] He believed the battle could have been avoided if only Pompey had agreed to talk with him.

During the night, some fifteen thousand of Pompey's soldiers retreated about six miles. By morning, however, they were so exhausted that they surrendered themselves. Pompey's grand army had been crushed. As in the past, Caesar showed mercy. Some of Pompey's officers he had captured before. They had promised not to take up arms against him again. These dishonorable men he ordered put to death. But Caesar allowed each of his soldiers the right to save one prisoner, perhaps an old friend or relative. He invited most of the captured soldiers to join his army. He was very glad to find Marcus Brutus, the son of his mistress Servilia, alive among the prisoners.

POMPEY'S HEAD

The battle of Pharsalus marked a turning point in the civil war. It was true Pompey's fleets still controlled much of the Mediterranean Sea. Pompey's republican allies still controlled Africa. Caesar had more work to do. He immediately set out after Pompey.

In September, Caesar crossed into Asia (present-day western Turkey). There, he learned that Pompey was hurrying to Egypt. Caesar crossed to the island of Rhodes and soon set sail for Alexandria, Egypt. In his haste, Caesar took with him just one small legion of about thirty-two hundred men. On the evening of October 1, 48 B.C., ship lookouts spied a burning light far in the distance. It was the famous lighthouse of Pharos at the entrance of Alexandria's harbor.

Pompey had hoped to find safety in Egypt. He had planned to ask its young king, Ptolemy XIII, for military help. He reached Alexandria just three days before Caesar. Hoping to win Caesar's favor, Ptolemy and his advisers ordered Pompey murdered. As Pompey was being rowed to shore, an Egyptian officer stabbed him to death in the boat.

When Caesar reached Alexandria on October 2, Theodotos, tutor to the boy-king, boarded Caesar's ship. He announced that King Ptolemy had a gift of welcome to give Caesar. A slave stepped forward carrying a wrapped bundle on a tray. Theodotos pulled back the cloth and revealed Pompey's bloody head. Caesar turned away at the sight. At one time Pompey had been Caesar's good friend and political ally. He had even been Caesar's son-in-law. Caesar ordered that Pompey's remains be returned to Italy to be buried with honor on Pompey's Alban estate. The tomb still stands today, in the public gardens of Albano, Italy.

⚔ PTOLEMY AND CLEOPATRA

Egypt was not a province of Rome. It was an independent kingdom ruled for centuries by the Ptolemy family. The first Ptolemy had been one of Alexander the Great's generals. Caesar quickly realized that Egypt was a country of great wealth. Alexandria was one of the largest cities in the world, with a population of more than half a million. The fertile soil along the banks of the Nile River yielded huge crops of grain each year. Clearly, it would be valuable to bring the kingdom under closer Roman control. Caesar decided he would try to do so.

At the time, there was unrest in Egypt. By command of King Ptolemy XII's will, his daughter Cleopatra VII and his son Ptolemy XIII were to share the throne. In 48 B.C., Cleopatra was twenty-one years old and Ptolemy thirteen. The boy's royal counselors did not want to share their power with Cleopatra. They drove her into exile. When Caesar arrived in Alexandria, he learned that Cleopatra was trying to return to Egypt at the head of a Syrian army.

Caesar offered to settle the civil war between Ptolemy and Cleopatra. He ordered both brother and sister to give up command of their armies and meet him in Alexandria. Ptolemy soon presented himself at the royal palace, but he kept his troops on alert. Cleopatra could not safely pass through Ptolemy's army lines to reach the city.

The writer Plutarch tells the following story:

> One evening at sunset, a small boat entered Alexandria
> Harbor and tied up near the royal palace. A Greek from

Sicily named Apollodorus stepped onto the dock. Over his shoulder, he carried a long, heavy bag. He brought the bag into the palace. It was a gift, he said, for Caesar. The bag was placed at Caesar's feet. In a moment, it began to wriggle and open. The bag came untied and out of it rose Cleopatra herself. With a smile, the young queen apologized for choosing this unusual manner of entering the palace. She could think of no other way to fulfill Caesar's summons.[23]

The girl's cleverness greatly affected Caesar. "The charm of her presence was irresistible," recorded Plutarch afterwards, "and there was an attractiveness in her person and talk . . ."[24] It was as if she had cast an instant spell over the Roman general. Fifty-two-year-old Caesar and twenty-one-year-old Cleopatra soon became lovers. They shared a real affection for one another, as well as similar political goals. Caesar decided to take her side in the civil war against her brother.

CAESAR AND CLEOPATRA

When Ptolemy discovered that Caesar favored his sister, he angrily left the palace. The boy-king's counselors and supporters soon appeared in the city streets. In public speeches, they excited Egyptian crowds. Soon Caesar and his single legion of thirty-two hundred men were besieged in the palace by an Egyptian mob. Within weeks, Ptolemy's entire army entered the city to join the fight. Caesar and his troops blocked the streets outside the palace with wagons, furniture, and whatever else they could find. They prepared to defend themselves.

The Egyptian general Achillas tried to storm the palace on November 10. But Caesar's stubborn soldiers fought off the attack.

For the next few weeks Caesar remained in a very dangerous situation. By boat and by land, he sent out brave messengers. He called upon loyal Roman generals and eastern allies for warships and reinforcements. Cleopatra stayed by his side in the palace. Finally, a Roman fleet arrived outside the harbor with two additional Roman legions. Caesar now felt strong enough to lead his troops out of the palace. They boldly set fire to the Egyptian fleet in the harbor and successfully burned most of it. Then they landed on the island of Pharos and captured the great lighthouse. In the meantime, the fire burning the Egyptian ships spread to the harbor docks. More than four hundred thousand papyrus scrolls stored on the docks went up in flames. Many valuable writings were lost forever. Stories passed down through the ages have suggested that Caesar burned the great library of Alexandria. But, in truth, the harbor fire was a good distance away from the library.[25]

Caesar now controlled both ends of Alexandria Harbor. But the Egyptians still held the Heptastadion. This was the harbor roadway that connected the island of Pharos with the city. Caesar boldly attempted to capture the Heptastadion in a naval battle. The Egyptians, however, overwhelmed his little force. Caesar jumped into a small boat in an effort to go to the aid of some of his men. He soon found himself nearly surrounded, however. He dove into the water, as enemy arrows pierced the waves around him. Luckily, he managed to

Cleopatra was Caesar's ally and lover. She later had an even closer relationship with Marc Antony. This portrait of Cleopatra was painted by the Italian Renaissance artist Michelangelo over fourteen hundred years after her death.

climb aboard another boat, but the Roman attack on the Heptastadion proved a failure.

By the middle of February 47 B.C., a messenger at last brought welcome news. Caesar's ally, Mithridates of Pergamum (present-day western Turkey) was marching to Egypt at the head of a large army. The army contained troops from Cilicia, Syria, Arabia, and also three thousand Jews. Caesar was able to sail out of Alexandria in order to join his approaching friends. On March 27, 47 B.C., Ptolemy's Egyptian army was defeated. While trying to escape capture, young King Ptolemy drowned in the Nile River. Caesar returned immediately to

Alexandria. Six months after his arrival in Egypt, Caesar restored Queen Cleopatra to her throne.

VENI, VIDI, VICI

Caesar had spent a lot of time in Egypt. He had wasted much of the advantage he had won at Pharsalus. Many Italians were grumbling about Marc Antony's leadership there. From his kingdom on the Black Sea, Pharnaces, the son of Mithridates, had invaded Pontus (present-day northern Turkey). In Africa, republicans Metellus Scipio and Marcus Cato were raising a large new army to resist Caesar. In Spain, Pompey's supporters were in open revolt. Throughout the Roman world there was still no peace. Yet, after placing Cleopatra on the Egyptian throne, Caesar remained at her side. In fact, during this time, he took a long pleasure trip with her. Cleopatra's royal barge measured three hundred feet long, forty-five feet wide, and sixty feet high. For weeks, Caesar relaxed aboard this ship. He and Cleopatra cruised along the Nile River as far as Ethiopia.

The love affair between Caesar and Cleopatra seemed real, and soon Cleopatra became pregnant. In the end, however, Caesar understood that duty called him. With a single, small legion, he set off for Syria at the end of May 47 B.C.

Caesar had decided to turn his attention first to Mithridates' son Pharnaces. He could not permit Pharnaces to regain his father's kingdom. All of Rome's control in the east might collapse. From Syria, Caesar hurried his forces north. At Zela, in the kingdom of

Pontus, Caesar fought Pharnaces on August 2, 47 B.C. The battle was so swift and his victory so complete that Caesar proudly would later tell a friend in Latin, "Veni, vidi, vici." In translation, the words are simple and direct: "I came, I saw, I conquered."[26]

A RETURN TO ROME

It was more than a year since the battle of Pharsalus. Caesar finally returned to Italy in October 47 B.C. In Rome, he held elections to fill government offices for the next year. He arranged for himself and loyal general Marcus Aemilus Lepidus to be elected consuls. Marcus Brutus, the son of his mistress Servilia, was made governor of Cisalpine Gaul.

Caesar sold Pompey's estates, as well as those of other dead or still rebellious enemy nobles. The money would pay his own troops and enable him to continue the civil war. To feed Rome's hungry poor, Caesar ordered that grain, cooking oil, and money be handed out.

Caesar also dealt with a mutiny among his soldiers. The troops of the XIIth Legion and the Xth Legion were both unhappy. Caesar suddenly appeared at the army camp on the Campus Martius to confront the problem. Officers explained that their men wished to be released. They insisted Caesar pay them the rewards he had promised them earlier in the war. After a long silence, Caesar told the assembled soldiers he would release them from further service. They would even receive their rewards. However, they would have to wait until he returned from Africa. There he would win glorious victory with his other legions. "I shall give you all that I have promised," he declared, "when I triumph with other soldiers."[27] Caesar's words filled his listeners with shame. They loved their general, and now they shouted that he should take them with him to Africa. Finally, he agreed. By the force of his personality, Caesar had turned a mutiny into a war rally.

War in Africa

After just two months in Rome, Caesar set off for Africa. The Roman province of Africa only covered a northern region of present-day Africa and included much of present-day Tunisia. By December 17, 47 B.C., Caesar arrived on the island of Sicily. He set sail a week later with six legions and two thousand cavalrymen. During the voyage, a terrible storm scattered Caesar's fleet. He landed with only three thousand soldiers and less than two hundred horsemen near the town of Hadrumetum (present-day Sousse in Tunisia). These troops wondered if fate was against them. Caesar had stumbled while stepping ashore. He had fallen to his knees. Caesar tried to turn a bad omen into a bold prediction. According to the writer Suetonius, he exclaimed, "I take possession of thee, Africa," and grasped the earth with his hands.[28]

Caesar's enemies had been busy in Africa. General Scipio had gathered ten republican Roman legions. There were another four legions of African allies commanded by King Juba of Numidia. Fifteen thousand cavalrymen also awaited orders.

Caesar sent urgent orders to Sicily. He needed the rest of his army and supplies. In the meantime, without enough grain or grass, Caesar found a way to feed his cavalry horses. Plutarch later explained, "He was forced to feed the horses with seaweed, which he washed . . . to take off its saltness, and mixed with a little grass to give it a more agreeable taste."[29] In time, ships began to arrive carrying additional troops and supplies. As the days passed, Caesar's army grew to a total of nearly thirty thousand men.

By April 6, 46 B.C., Caesar was ready to fight. He marched to the outskirts of the town of Thapsus. Both Caesar's and Scipio's armies prepared to give battle on the sandy plain. Then, something unexpected happened. Eager troops on Caesar's right wing forced their trumpeter to sound the charge. Without orders from Caesar, his entire army rushed forward toward the enemy. Caesar could not hold back his excited troops. All he could do was join the attack, galloping his horse ahead toward the battleline.

Scipio's army possessed African elephants. Caesar's archers and slingers sent a stinging rain of arrows and stones down upon the giant beasts. The wounded animals finally turned around and stampeded among their own troops. The enemy cavalry fled in complete disorder. Caesar's soldiers charged through Scipio's camp and then King Juba's. Stunned enemy troops dropped their weapons in surrender. The war frenzy of Caesar's men could not be stopped. Over ten thousand surrendering men were slaughtered. General Scipio and King Juba later chose to commit suicide rather than be

The Falling Sickness

Some scholars believe Caesar took no active part in the Battle of Thapsus. The Roman writer Plutarch, for example, reported that "While he was drawing up his army in battle order he is said to have been overcome by his usual sickness."[30] He felt a physical illness coming on and had himself taken away. The "usual sickness" is thought to have been epilepsy. The Roman biographer Suetonius wrote of Caesar, "In his later days he was given to faint and swoon suddenly. . . . he was surprised with the falling sickness."[31]

captured. Caesar's victory at Thapsus allowed him to bring part of Juba's kingdom under Roman control for the first time. Carved out of Numidia, Caesar gave Rome a new province to be called Africa Nova.

After the battle, Caesar marched north to the coastal city of Utica. Caesar's old Senate enemy Marcus Cato commanded the republican force there. Cato recognized his hopeless situation. He also chose suicide by falling on his own sword rather than surrender.

Caesar's war in Africa had ended. In the spring of 46 B.C., he journeyed back to Rome. On the way, he stopped to visit the island of Sardinia. By July 46 B.C., Caesar was back in Rome. He called upon all citizens to unite in peace once more. The Senate voted Caesar a public thanksgiving of forty days for his victory at Thapsus. This was a celebration twice as long as the one he had enjoyed after Alesia.

DICTATOR

During September 46 B.C., Rome held a series of four spectacular triumphs. The triumphs honored Caesar for the great victories he had won on foreign soil: Gaul, Egypt, Pontus (Asia), and Africa. The treasure used to pay for these celebrations included 2,822 gold crowns presented by towns and cities throughout the Roman Empire. Their total weight was 20,414 pounds.[1]

"REMEMBER YOU ARE HUMAN"

Each grand parade began on the Campus Martius. It passed through the city and ended at the Temple of Jupiter. Guarded wagons rolled through the crowded streets carrying gold and other captured treasures. Slaves carried paintings showing scenes of Caesar's many battles. Lists of killed and captured enemies and maps of conquered territories were displayed. Behind these, Caesar's most important war prisoners were marched. They included Vercingetorix and Juba's four-year-old son. Caesar's triumphs proclaimed the glory of Rome. Rome now possessed an empire that stretched from the Rhine River in the north to the African desert in the south.

After the parade of prisoners came a long line of lictors. They were followed by Caesar himself. He rode in a fabulous chariot pulled by four white horses. Each horse wore a crown. Caesar was dressed in a purple toga. A laurel wreath crowned his head. He held an eagle scepter in his hand. His face was painted red. The honored victor was supposed to resemble Jupiter, king of the gods. Romans believed that it was Jupiter who had made Rome's armies successful. Behind Caesar on his chariot stood a slave. The slave held a golden wreath over Caesar's head. Another slave walked behind the chariot chanting, "Remember you are human."[2] This was to keep Caesar from becoming too proud and making the gods jealous. It was the custom at triumphs.

Each triumphant march took up an entire day. At the end of the last parade, a huge banquet was served. Two hundred thousand Roman citizens feasted at twenty-two thousand tables. Then came a series of grand events. Romans were treated to the most amazing entertainments ever seen in the city. Caesar presented boxing matches, plays, and chariot races. Gladiators fought lions in the Roman Circus. The final event was the most spectacular. Two armies battled one another for public enjoyment. War prisoners were matched against condemned Roman criminals. For five days, fights were held that included as many as five hundred foot soldiers, twenty elephants, and thirty horsemen on each side. The prisoners and criminals were forced to fight each other to the death.

FURTHER HONORS

In September 46 B.C., Cleopatra arrived in Rome. She brought with her the one-year-old son she had had with Caesar. She had named him Caesarion. Caesar gave his Egyptian lover a villa outside the city limits in which to live while she visited.

The Senate heaped honors upon Caesar. They could hardly resist the wishes of such a powerful man. Caesar was granted the right to an escort of seventy-two lictors. No Roman ever had received such a great honor. The Senate ordered that a statue of Caesar standing on a globe be placed in the Temple of Jupiter. The statue symbolized Caesar's military might. Caesar's golden triumphal chariot was also brought to the temple for his

At the height of his power, Caesar became dictator of Rome.

use. The Senate proclaimed Caesar Rome's dictator for the next ten years. The Senate further granted him the right to sit beside the consuls in the Senate. He would be recognized first in all Senate debates.

Caesar immediately took control of the government. He reorganized government offices throughout Italy. New laws would create local government centers in farming districts. Every Italian town and territory would obey Roman law. He also reduced the office terms of provincial governors, reformed court proceedings, and increased the penalties for some crimes.

Faced with huge expenses, Caesar snatched up every source of income that he could find. Rich men and entire cities in Asia, Spain, and Egypt were heavily taxed. Caesar took possession of all of the property of his enemies. Their lands, houses, and furniture were used to pay off Caesar's supporters or to enrich himself.

No one fully understood how much power Caesar planned to take. Cicero remarked that "no one should be able to do more than the laws and the Senate."[3] He and others hoped Caesar would respect Rome's republican values. Caesar, in fact, did make speeches to the Senate and the people. He tried to calm their fears. But there could be no mistake. Caesar possessed so much power that nothing could be done unless he wanted it done.

KEEPING PEOPLE EMPLOYED

Above all things, Caesar intended to take care of his army veterans. They deserved to be rewarded for their loyalty and good service on the battlefield. He began by granting them each a bonus of twenty thousand sesterces. It was a huge amount of money. His soldiers could live in comfort the rest of their lives.

Next, he looked for ways to put tens of thousands of Romans to work in the city and throughout Italy. He planned the construction of a new Senate-House. It would replace the building burned down after the death of Clodius. Plans to build new canals in Italy and Greece would employ thousands. He also suggested dredging the harbor at Ostia. By deepening the harbor, ships would be allowed greater use of the Tiber River. Still another of Caesar's projects was to drain the Pomptine marshes. These marshlands covered some forty miles of the coastal region south of Rome.

Rome already had aqueducts. These high man-made channels carried water from the countryside to the city. Caesar made plans for another. He would tunnel into a large mountain lake in central Italy and add more fresh water to the city's water supply. It was a project that would employ some thirty thousand workers for more than twenty years. In addition, he desired the construction of more roads throughout Italy. This would keep thousands of army veterans employed. He was certain the old soldiers who had built the Rhine bridges and siege works in Gaul could also build fine roads.

IMPROVING ROMAN LIFE

Caesar had always been interested in books and learning. Now he made it clear he wished to make Rome a center of learning and culture as great as Alexandria.

MALA ARIA

By draining the Pomptine marshes, Caesar hoped to cure a major health problem in the region. It was commonly thought the marshes gave off "mala aria" (bad air). Terentius Varro, a scholar in Rome, stated his belief that "in the neighborhood of swamps . . . there are bred certain . . . creatures which cannot be seen by the eyes, which float in the air and enter the body through the mouth and nose and hereby cause serious diseases."[4] Of course, it is known today that the disease malaria is carried by mosquitoes.

Therefore, he appointed the scholar Varro to establish Rome's first public library. As chief librarian, Varro was instructed to assemble a fine collection of Greek and Latin books. In his quest for knowledge, Caesar also commissioned four Greek geographers to create a map of the entire world as carefully as possible. That difficult job would not be finished for another twenty years. Further, to promote intellectual activity in Rome, Caesar offered citizenship to all foreign teachers and doctors who would settle in the city. Caesar also allowed religious freedom in the city. He gave Rome's large Jewish population the right to practice their faith.

Caesar's new calendar was an important change in daily Roman life. It was designed by the Greek astronomer Sosigenes of Alexandria. Rome's old calendar was a lunar calendar. It measured time by the changing phases of the moon. The lunar calendar only had 355 days in a year. To keep up with the changing seasons, an extra month had to be added every other year. During the civil war, Caesar, as high priest, had failed to keep the calendar up to date. As a result, the seasons had shifted. The harvest festival no longer took place in the summer. It occurred in the fall. The grape-picking celebrations no longer took place in the fall. They took place in the chill of early winter. Rome's lunar calendar had fallen ninety days behind the weather.

The new calendar Caesar settled upon was a solar calendar. It measured the year based on the time it took the earth to circle the sun. Even this calendar was not perfect. It failed to calculate the earth's entire journey by eleven minutes. In 1582 A.D., Pope Gregory XIII would make a slight adjustment in the calculations. Today, however, Caesar's adjusted calendar is still the one that is used by much of the world.

It seemed the civil war had ended, and Caesar was supreme. He had himself elected to a fifth consulship in 45 B.C. There were Roman nobles who agreed that Caesar displayed charm and goodwill in the Senate. It was true he kept law and order in Rome. But no one on earth had ever been so powerful. Romans wondered what the future held under the leadership of such a man.

THE SPANISH REVOLT

Caesar had been in Rome only eight months when he found it necessary to return to Spain. In Spain, Pompey's sons, Gnaeus and Sextus, had raised thirteen legions against him.

Caesar first marched to the enemy stronghold of Ategua. On February 19, 45 B.C., after a siege of two months, the city surrendered. Next, Caesar captured and fortified the town of Munda, forty miles east of present-day Seville. On March 17, the army of Pompey's sons arrived outside the town walls. Caesar promptly ordered that his battle flag be displayed. He placed the Xth Legion on the right flank of his battle line. The IIIrd and Vth Legions stood on the left. When his preparations were complete, he started his army marching across the five-mile plain outside of the town.

The enemy troops awaited the impact of the attack. Just as they had at Thapsus, Caesar's soldiers excitedly charged into battle without orders. This time, however, the enemy stood firm. The force of the attack could not break the enemy battle line. Caesar's army began to falter. "Caesar, seeing his men hard pressed," wrote Plutarch, "and making but a weak resistance, ran through the ranks among the soldiers . . ."[5] He grabbed a shield from one of his soldiers and waded into the fray. He shouted, "Aren't you ashamed to hand me over to these boys?"[6] By this, he meant Pompey's sons. He threw off his helmet, so that his men could recognize him as their leader.

Caesar's words and his personal example turned the tide of the battle at Munda. In the end, the enemy lost some thirty thousand soldiers. By a miracle, Caesar's officers reported losses of no more than a thousand men. Caesar had had a close call at Munda. "When he came back from the fight," Plutarch later remarked, "he told his friends that he had often fought for victory, but this was the first time he had ever fought for life."[7] In the days that followed, other Spanish towns were captured. At the start of April, Gnaeus Pompey was killed. The rebellion in Spain had been crushed.

CAESAR TRIUMPHANT

By October 45 B.C., the dictator had returned to Rome. To honor Caesar's latest victory, the Senate declared a thanksgiving period of fifty days. He was awarded another triumph. Statues of Caesar appeared throughout Rome. One statue was inscribed "To the invincible god" and placed in the Forum.[8] Others appeared in Rome's many temples. In cities throughout the empire, Caesar's statue was displayed in places where proper respect could be shown. This was done by order of the Senate.

The government also minted a new coin. On it was a portrait of Caesar. It was the first time in Roman history a living person appeared on a coin. Caesar's birthday was declared a day of public celebration. The month Quintilis, his birth month, was renamed Julius (today July) to honor him even further. The Senate awarded Caesar a golden chair. He sat on it during court hearings and at Senate meetings. The Senate also agreed that any new law Caesar wanted did not require a vote to pass.

Caesar now saw the great need to retire as many of his soldiers as possible. The government could not support thirty-five legions in peacetime. Caesar began distributing plots of land to his veterans throughout Italy. At the same time, he decided on another method to solve Rome's constant poverty problem. He gave land away to many poor Romans in far away provinces. Nearly forty new colonies sprang up in Gaul, Spain, Africa, Syria, and elsewhere. So many settlers left Rome that Caesar lowered the unemployment rolls from 320,000 to 150,000.[9]

Caesar decided to raise the membership in the Senate from about six hundred to nine hundred. Many of the new senators were Caesar's loyal followers. The increase in number allowed Caesar to reward young officers, Gauls, and others who owed their Roman citizenship to him. In fact, almost half of the new senators came from places other than Rome or Italy. Suddenly Rome's old noble families were forced to accept strange foreigners as equals. "Mongrel Gauls no better than half barbarians, he admitted to senatorial degree," declared the writer Suetonius.[10] Caesar needed the continued support of these men. "Even if," he remarked, "in defense of my position, I had been obliged to call upon the services of bandits and cut-throats, I should have given them their rewards."[11]

Rome's noblemen watched bitterly as Caesar made these changes. They had once made the government's decisions. Now they could do no more than agree to Caesar's wishes. For 44 B.C., Caesar arranged that he and Marc Antony would be elected consuls. The defeat of Crassus in the desert of Syria still required revenge. Caesar wanted to add the enemy kingdom of Parthia to the empire. Therefore, he decided to lead a campaign against the Parthians. In January 44 B.C., Caesar announced that he would give his place as consul to Publius Cornelius Dolabella before leaving for the Parthian war. According to the old Roman law, Marc Antony and Dolabella were too young to become consuls. Marc Antony was about thirty-eight and Dolabella was no more than twenty-five years old. But by now, if Caesar wished it, it was done.

10

THE IDES OF MARCH

On February 14, 44 B.C., the Senate voted Caesar the title of dictator for life. "I have lived long enough for both nature and fame," Caesar had once admitted.[1] All of his life, Caesar had been a man of almost constant energy. Now, the fifty-six-year-old leader had begun to show signs of old age. Still vain, Caesar combed his hair forward so that it covered his balding head.

There was another change in his behavior that Romans noticed. He seemed to be setting himself high above his fellow nobles. In the Senate, he often wore a purple toga and a jewel-encrusted golden wreath on his head. Sometimes, he also wore high red boots. The ancient kings of the Alban district of Italy had worn such boots as a sign of their royalty.

THE FESTIVAL OF THE LUPERCAL

On February 15, 44 B.C., Romans celebrated the ancient Festival of the Lupercal. It was a day to honor the founding of Rome. After a sacrifice of goats and a dog, the priests of the Luperci smeared their faces with the animal blood. Then they danced and ran a race through the streets dressed in little more than wolfskins. That day, in the Forum, high on a platform Caesar sat on his golden chair, dressed in his purple toga.

Marc Antony was one of the Lupercal racers. "Antony, as consul," explained Plutarch, "was one of those who ran this course, and when he came into the Forum . . . the people made way for him . . ."[2] When he reached Caesar, Marc Antony rushed up to him and offered him a golden crown. Three times Marc Antony presented the crown, and three times Caesar refused to accept it. "Jupiter alone is King of the Romans," Caesar declared.[3] At last, Caesar took the crown and threw it into the crowd below him. Yet it was whispered among many Romans that Caesar really did want to be king.

In the days that followed, Caesar continued his plans for his Parthian war. He had decided he would leave Rome on March 18. He expected his new war campaign would last three years.

Noble Plotters

There were men in Rome who hated Caesar. During the civil war, Caesar had killed in battle the family and friends of some nobles. Other noblemen survived the war by accepting Caesar's mercy. That fact insulted their senses of honor and dignity. In addition, some of Caesar's closest supporters felt he had not properly rewarded them. Ambitious men, bitter men, and men who truly believed in the Roman Republic, all had reasons to wish Caesar dead. It is not surprising, then, that a group of nobles had begun to plot against Caesar.

The two leaders of the plot were Gaius Cassius Longinus and his brother-in-law Marcus Junius Brutus. Brutus was Cato's son-in-law. His mother was Caesar's favorite mistress, Servilia. Gossips even falsely whispered that Caesar might be his father.

Decimus Brutus (a distant relation of Marcus Brutus) had been one of Caesar's best officers in Gaul. Decimus Brutus joined the plot, too. He felt a greater loyalty to his noble class than to Caesar. Casca, Cimber Tullus, and Gaius Trebonius also agreed to help. Altogether, perhaps sixty nobles joined the plot. These men secretly decided Caesar must be murdered. They believed that if Caesar were not stopped he would become a king. They believed that only with his death could the Republic be restored. The ancient writer Nicolaus of Damascus later explained:

> Thus there were leagued against him men of every condition, great and small, friends and enemies, soldiers and civilians. . . . The meetings at which they laid their plans were never held openly of course. They would go secretly, a few at a time, to one or another's house, and at those gatherings they discussed many different proposals . . .[4]

Finally, Caesar announced he would attend the Senate on March 15, 44 B.C. It would be the last time he would appear in public before leaving for Parthia. The plotters seized on this appearance as the last chance to carry out their deadly plan.

PREMONITIONS OF DEATH

Some time earlier, Caesar had dismissed his Spanish bodyguard. Until then, two thousand loyal soldiers had gone with him wherever he went. Caesar was urged by friends to keep the Spaniards. But he declared, "There is no worse fate than to be continuously protected, for that means you are in constant fear."[5]

On the evening of March 14, Caesar dined at the home of his friend Marcus Lepidus. The guests stretched out on couches and drank wine mixed with water. Caesar never wasted time. During the long meal, he read and signed letters. He also listened to the conversation around him. At one point, someone wondered what would be the best death for a man. Caesar insisted that the best death was a sudden and unexpected one.[6]

That night, Caesar lay in bed beside his wife Calpurnia. Suddenly, a gust of wind blew open the bedroom doors and windows. Caesar, surprised by the noise, sat up in his bed. In the moonlight, he saw that Calpurnia was fast asleep. But she was groaning and mumbling words. When she woke up, she described an awful dream. She had been holding Caesar's murdered body in her arms. She had been crying over it.[7]

In the morning, Calpurnia begged her husband to stay at home. She told him he must not go to the meeting of the Senate. Her words startled Caesar. She had never been superstitious about anything before. But now she clearly feared for his life. Her dream had upset her greatly. Caesar consulted priests who made animal sacrifices. The priests told him that they saw unlucky signs in the organs of the animals. Caesar himself did not feel well that day. At last, he decided to send for Marc Antony and to dismiss the Senate. It was then that the plotter Decimus Brutus arrived at Caesar's home. Decimus Brutus made arguments why Caesar must attend the meeting. "At the last," the writer Suetonius later recorded, "being . . . persuaded by Decimus Brutus not to disappoint the senators who were now in full assembly . . . he went forth when it was well near eleven of the clock."[8]

LAST WARNINGS

On March 15, 44 B.C., the Senate assembled in the great hall that was part of Pompey's theatre. Since the burning of the old Senate-House, the Senate was still meeting there. Caesar arrived late. Servants carried him there on a litter. A couch with a roof and carrying poles, a litter was city transportation for the rich. At last, Caesar rose from his litter to walk into Pompey's theatre. It was then that he was approached by a man named Artemidorus of Cnidos. Artemidorus was a teacher of Greek philosophy. He was friendly with Brutus and some of the other plotters and had learned of their plan.

Artemidorus carried a scroll that would reveal the plot to Caesar. Caesar was surrounded by people. Many were thrusting petitions into his hands. Caesar, in turn, handed these documents to his attendants to be examined later. When Artemidorus gave Caesar his scroll, he insisted, "Read this Caesar, alone, and quickly, for it contains matter of great importance which . . .

concerns you."[9] Caesar kept the written warning in his hand. Several times he was about to read it. But so many people approached to speak to him, he never had the chance. He carried the scroll with him as he made his way toward the Senate hall.

Just outside the Senate door, something else happened. Spurrina was a soothsayer. He was a fortune-teller who had earlier told Caesar to beware of the Ides of March. Now Caesar spied Spurrina standing near the doorway, watching his progress. Caesar smiled at the sight of him. "The day which you warned me against is here, and I am still alive," Caesar remarked. "Yes," Spurrina gravely answered, "It is here—but it is not yet past."[10] Caesar did not guess the importance of his words. He entered the Senate hall.

ASSASSINATION

Carrying out their plan, Gaius Trebonius kept Marc Antony in conversation outside the hall. The plotters did not want Caesar's loyal, muscular friend by his side when they attacked. As Caesar passed among them, the senators rose from their seats. Caesar walked to his golden chair and sat down. The chair was positioned before a statue of Pompey at the front of the room. Some of the plotters were already standing behind the chair. Others stepped forward, as if they wanted to speak with Caesar.

"Cimber Tullus," wrote Suetonius later, "who had undertaken to begin first, stepped nearer unto him, as though he would have made some request."[11] Cimber Tullus had a brother who was in exile. He asked that Caesar pardon his brother and let him return home. Other plotters closed in, pretending to support Cimber Tullus in his request. Caesar replied that he would not grant the pardon.

Suddenly, Cimber Tullus grabbed hold of Caesar's toga. He pulled it down from Caesar's neck with both of his hands. This was the agreed upon signal for the deadly attack to begin.

The historian Suetonius tells us that Caesar exclaimed, "This is violence!"[12]

Casca then drew his dagger and struck the first nervous blow. It cut Caesar slightly on the neck. Caesar quickly turned and seized hold of the weapon.

According to the writer Plutarch, Caesar shouted, "Vile Casca, what does this mean?"

"Brother, help," Casca called out to his brother.[13]

Most of the assembled senators stared in horror. Those in the conspiracy, however, drew their knives and attacked. They had pledged that every plotter must strike Caesar at least once. Caesar whirled left and right, trying to avoid the blows. He received at least twenty-three stab wounds. Out of the attacking mob, Marcus Brutus stepped forward and stabbed Caesar in the groin. Caesar saw his face in the ugly crowd. "You too, my boy?" he gasped.[14] He felt especially betrayed by Brutus whom he had favored. The writer Appian later declared, "With rage and shouts Caesar turned, like a wild animal, upon each of them, but after Brutus' blow he at last gave up, covered his head with his toga and fell with dignity by the statue of Pompey. Even so they continued to rain blows upon the fallen body."[15] Finally the bloody deed was done.

"Long live the Republic!" yelled the assassins. "The tyrant is dead."[16]

Brutus turned to the shocked senators who had witnessed the murder. He tried to explain to them the

Caesar was stabbed repeatedly by his attackers.

reasons for the killing. No one would listen. In panic, the senators fled the building. They shouted the awful news in the streets. They rushed to their homes and locked their doors. This was revolution. Who could guess who would be murdered next? What would happen next? At last, Caesar's bloody body lay alone in the empty Senate hall. "Three slaves," recorded Appian afterwards, "the only ones to stay behind, put the corpse on a litter and unsteadily, since they were only three, they carried home the man who a little earlier had been ruler of land and sea."[17]

CAESAR'S FUNERAL

As word of Caesar's assassination spread, Romans lived in fear and wonder. The Senate met again on March 16. To calm Caesar's many supporters, it was voted in the Senate that all laws passed by Caesar would be kept without change. It was also revealed that Marc Antony's life had been spared. Brutus argued that this mercy showed that the plotters had no desire to overthrow the government. Marc Antony came out of hiding when he learned he would not be killed. He insisted that Caesar receive a public funeral. He demanded that Caesar's will be read for all to hear. The Senate agreed.

That day, March 16, Brutus addressed a large crowd in the Forum. Again, he tried to explain the reasons Caesar had been killed. His speech had little impact. Later that day, Caesar's body was carried into the Forum. Marc Antony stepped onto the speaker's platform to give a funeral speech to the gathered crowd.

First, he revealed the contents of Caesar's will. It showed Caesar's love for the people. In his will, Caesar had left a gift of three hundred sesterces to every voting Roman citizen. He also gave the people his private gardens beyond the Tiber River to be used as public parks.

Marc Antony then turned to where Caesar's body lay on the platform beside him. He spoke words in favor of Caesar to excite the emotions of his listeners. He stripped Caesar's toga from the corpse. It was stiff with blood. He unfolded it and pointed out where every knife had cut through. He even raised the toga on a pole, so

WILLIAM SHAKESPEARE'S JULIUS CAESAR

William Shakespeare (1564–1616) is regarded by many as the greatest playwright in the English language. In 1599, Shakespeare penned an historical play entitled *The Tragedy of Julius Caesar*. The play describes the events leading up to the assassination of Caesar and the death of Brutus afterwards. One of the most thrilling passages in all of Shakespeare's writings is Marc Antony's speech over the body of Caesar. It includes the following words:

Friends, Romans, countrymen, lend me your ears.
I come to bury Caesar, not to praise him.
The evil that men do lives after them,
The good is oft interred with their bones.
So let it be with Caesar. The noble Brutus
Hath told you Caesar was ambitious.
If it were so, it was a grievous fault,
And grievously hath Caesar answered it.[18]

people at the back of the crowded Forum could see. At last, the crowd lost all control.

"Kill Brutus, kill Cassius!" men and women shouted with tears in their eyes.[19]

Full of grief, the frenzied mob grabbed benches and tables from neighborhood shops. They threw them into a pile to make a funeral pyre. They lay Caesar's corpse on this and set it ablaze. The flames rose high into the air. Black smoke drifted through the streets. Today in Rome, in the ruins of the Forum, the simple brick Temple of Julius Caesar still stands. According to legend, it is on that spot that Caesar's remains were burned and buried.[20]

While the fired burned, people rushed close and seized hold of blazing wood to use as torches. They vowed revenge on Caesar's murderers. Shouting furiously, people surrounded the Senate-House. Because Caesar had been murdered there, they burned the building to the ground. Some angry Romans happened upon a tribune named Cinna. He had the same name as a Cinna who once had made a speech against Caesar. They gave the innocent man no chance to explain himself. They beat him to death and tore apart his fallen body.

Rome's rioting mobs convinced Brutus, Cassius, and the other plotters that the city was unsafe for them. Romans were not going to greet them as heroes anytime soon. Within a few days they escaped the city. They took refuge on their country estates. Caesar's assassination had left Rome with an uncertain future.

THE RISE OF AUGUSTUS

"If anything happens to me," Caesar had once predicted, "Rome will enjoy no peace. A new civil war will break out under far worse conditions than the last one."[1] His prediction was all too correct. The assassination of Caesar did not restore the Republic. It only started another terrible civil war.

OCTAVIUS BECOMES A CAESAR

In his will, Caesar left most of his wealth and property to his eighteen-year-old grandnephew Gaius Octavius Thurnius. He also adopted Gaius and gave him the name Octavian Caesar. Octavian had served on his granduncle's army staff in Spain. Although sickly, Octavian had shown himself tough and courageous. Caesar had grown very fond of him. He liked having his company and hearing his clever conversation.

In March 44 B.C., Octavian was studying at Apollonia across the Adriatic Sea. It was his plan to join Caesar in the Parthian war. He learned of Caesar's assassination in a letter from his mother. Octavian hurried back to Rome to claim his inheritance.

Octavian discovered he had a great deal of support in Rome. Thousands of army veterans wished revenge on Caesar's murderers. Many Roman nobles and commoners also saw Octavian as a better leader than Marc Antony. Cicero, for one, took a chance and gave young Octavian his political support. He hoped by doing this he would help ruin Marc Antony.

In January 43 B.C., Octavian was invited by the Senate to join their ranks. More important, he took command of Rome's republican army. The soldiers in Octavian's army were loyal old supporters of Julius Caesar. Once at the head of his troops, Octavian surprised the Senate. He asked to be elected consul. In July 43 B.C., the Senate refused his request. In response, Octavian marched his army into Rome. Worried senators changed their minds and welcomed him at the gates. On August 19, Octavian got his wish and became consul, just as Julius had been.

Sixteen months after arriving in Rome, Octavian arranged a meeting with Marc Antony and Marcus Lepidus. Lepidus, it will be remembered, was one of Julius Caesar's best generals and closest supporters. Octavian, Marc Antony, and Lepidus made an agreement to share power in Rome. Like Caesar, Pompey, and Crassus before them, they would join together in order to control the government. In 43 B.C., the Second Triumvirate was born. The historian Appian recorded, "Thus the three divided the Roman empire among themselves . . ."[2]

THE FATE OF THE ASSASSINS

Octavian, Marc Antony, and Lepidus were determined to bring Caesar's assassins to justice. Brutus and Cassius had escaped to Greece. They were raising an army there. Octavian and Marc Antony crossed the Adriatic Sea with a huge army of twenty-eight legions. In 42 B.C., they fought their enemies in two battles at Philippi. The army of Brutus and Cassius was defeated. Rather than be captured, Cassius soon committed suicide. Plutarch later claimed, "The most remarkable of . . . coincidences was that which befell Cassius, who, when he was defeated at Philippi, killed himself with the same dagger which he had made use of against Caesar."[3]

Brutus also chose to die rather than become a prisoner. It is said he had a young follower named Strabo hold a sword, point outward. Brutus then threw his body against it, so that the point pierced his chest. It seems all of Caesar's assassins were fated to die violently. The writer Suetonius later revealed, "Of those murderers, there was not one . . . that either survived him above three years, or died of his natural death. All stood condemned; and by one mishap or other perished, some by shipwreck, others in battle . . ."[4] Still others, like Brutus, Cassius, and the Casca brothers, committed suicide instead of facing justice.

A DIVIDED EMPIRE

The Second Triumvirate decided war should be fought against Parthia. This would strengthen Rome's power and prevent rebellion in the empire. Marc Antony agreed to lead a Roman army in that glorious task. He set off for the eastern provinces.

At the same time, Octavian remained in Rome. He worked on winning supporters in the Senate and building his own army. Marc Antony's wife Fulvia and his brother Lucius saw Octavian as a growing threat. They raised eight legions of their own in Italy. Octavian seized this chance to gain greater power. He sent his best general, Agrippa, to fight Lucius Antony. Agrippa besieged Lucius Antony's army in the Italian town of Perugia during the winter of 41–40 B.C. Octavian also used the opportunity provided by this civil war to take control of all of the Roman legions in Gaul.

To restore the peace and preserve their alliance, Marc Antony and Octavian made a new agreement. In the Treaty of Brindisi, it was decided Octavian would keep control of Gaul, Transalpine Gaul, and Cisalpine Gaul. Marc Antony would control Asia, Syria, and Rome's other eastern provinces. This treaty kept Rome

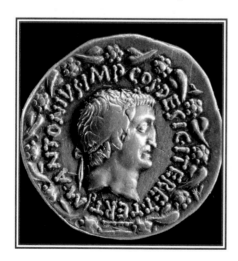

at peace for a while. In time, however, the Second Triumvirate fell apart. Then, in 36 B.C., Octavian placed Lepidus under arrest. It was

This coin showing Marc Antony was minted in celebration of the marriage of Antony to Octavia, who was Octavian's sister.

believed Lepidus was planning to join forces with Pompey's son Sextus. Together they hoped to claim Sicily as their own. Octavian allowed Lepidus to go into quiet retirement. But this development signaled the end of the Second Triumvirate. Now the battle for control of the Roman Empire was to be waged between Octavian and Marc Antony alone.

ANTONY AND CLEOPATRA

While Marc Antony remained in the east, Octavian strengthened his hold on Rome. To begin, he set upon a lifelong project of making the city more beautiful and grand. He ordered the city's old aqueducts repaired and new ones built. Cool mountain water bubbled up from the city's fountains. He put stone masons to work. Fabulous temples of marble began to rise up in place of old brick ones. In 34 B.C., Octavian arranged for his election as consul for the second time. He also was able to get Roman citizens to pledge loyalty to him.

In the east, Marc Antony had met Queen Cleopatra again. He had known her when she was Caesar's lover. In 37 B.C., she used her charms to become Antony's lover. It was a political arrangement as well. Antony needed Egypt's wealth to support his army. Cleopatra wanted Antony and his army to help her establish an empire of her own in Greece.

The alliance of Antony and Cleopatra finally caused Octavian to go to war against them in 31 B.C. The entire war was decided in a single battle. In September, Marc Antony met defeat in a naval fight outside the harbor of Actium, Greece. Antony escaped to Egypt with Cleopatra, but Octavian led an army after them. In time, Octavian besieged Alexandria and conquered the city.

Antony and Cleopatra realized that their futures were doomed. Antony committed suicide by falling on his sword because he had falsely heard that Cleopatra was dead. After Antony had died, Cleopatra chose a different death. She allowed a poisonous snake, an asp, to sink its fangs into her. She died of the poisonous bite. Afterward, Octavian returned to Rome in triumph. No Romans dared to challenge him now. At the age of thirty-four, Julius Caesar's adopted son had reached the heights of power.

AUGUSTUS CAESAR

In 35 B.C. Octavian announced to the Senate that the Republic was restored. He had made arrangements secretly before making this statement. On cue, his supporters in the Senate shouted that they would not let him give up his leadership. Instead, the Senate awarded Octavian the title of Augustus, meaning the great or grand one. Augustus wisely refused to give himself the title of emperor. That would anger too many nobles. But he was, in fact, an absolute ruler. In constant control, nothing would occur without his personal approval.

After 27 B.C., the Senate resumed its position as the Republic's advisor. But Augustus Caesar remained governor of almost all provinces where soldiers were stationed. As long as he commanded the armies, Augustus knew he controlled Rome. Finally, after ruling for forty-one

Augustus Caesar consolidated his power and became the first emperor of Rome.

years, he died at the age of seventy-five in 14 A.D. He had lived a life worthy of the name Caesar. Other emperors taking the name would follow after him.

LIFE AND LEGACY

It is difficult to imagine our world without the place Julius Caesar holds in it. It seems that from childhood it was Caesar's destiny to be great. Caesar's life was one he made for himself. The custom among Roman nobles was to win honor for one's family through public service. Caesar took this custom seriously. Ambition made success his life's quest.

Military tribune, quaestor, curator of the Appian Way, aedile, pontifex maximus, praetor, governor of Further Spain—Caesar held all of these offices. Still, he wanted more. He was ruthless in his desire to advance himself. He married women not for love but for wealth and political connections. In order to become consul, he bargained with Pompey and Crassus. The three men formed their Triumvirate and for a time shared all of the power that Rome could offer. By breaking Roman laws and customs, Consul Caesar had to sacrifice his honor. But by then his ambition had taken such a hold of him he did not seem to care.

141

Beginning in 58 B.C., Caesar set out upon the career that would truly make him great. By becoming the governor of Cisalpine Gaul, Transalpine Gaul, and Illyricum, Caesar also became a military leader. He immediately set out to prove himself a brilliant general. The unconquered territory of Gaul to the north provided him with his opportunity. During the next eight years, Caesar marched at the head of his legions. He successfully fought Gauls, Germans, and Britons. The constant news of Caesar's victories amazed Romans. Speed and boldness were the methods Caesar skillfully used. His ability to adapt to new situations and his willingness to take chances became legendary.

It is natural that the Roman Senate would both admire and fear a genius such as Caesar. The senators tried to remove Caesar as a threat. Their plan failed. Rather than give up his armies, Caesar plunged Rome into a long civil war. Again, Caesar triumphed over his enemies, but they were enemies he had wanted as friends. Caesar defeated Pompey at Pharsalus. Eventually, he won the civil war. He even took time to fight a war on behalf of his lover Cleopatra in Egypt.

The Senate named Caesar dictator for life. At the head of the government, Caesar tried to improve life for Romans. He distributed public land. He put army veterans and jobless Romans to work on building projects. Always a curious intellectual, Caesar founded a library and practiced religious tolerance. He embraced many new ideas, such as the Julian calendar.

As a man, Caesar could overwhelm people with the force of his character. He made himself into a wonderful public speaker. More than once, he won battles and put down mutinies by the commanding impact of his words. He was a man of personal courage, too. Repeatedly, he turned the tide of battle by bravely charging in among his soldiers.

Caesar was a man of constant energy and had varied interests. His book *The Gallic War* proved his skill as a writer. After fighting Pompey's army, he wrote another book called *The Civil War*. It was also well-written. When published together, *The Gallic War* and *The Civil War* are known as *Caesar's War Commentaries*.

Caesar had reached the greatest height of success. Common Romans marveled at all he had done. He had earned, however, the hatred of too many nobles. His disregard of ancient Roman customs and the republican ideal proved his undoing. On the Ides of March, 44 B.C., Caesar was assassinated.

The death of Caesar did not restore the Roman Republic. It only prepared the way for Augustus and the rise of the Roman Empire. After Caesar, Rome was ruled by emperors for the next five hundred years. They all called themselves Caesar. "Caesar was born to do great things, and had a passion after honor . . ." remarked the writer Plutarch.[5] To honor the greatness of the man, other European rulers would also take the name Caesar. In Germany, they called themselves Kaisers. In Russia, they were called Czars. No higher compliment could have been given him. In life and death, Julius Caesar had made his mark in history for all time.

CHRONOLOGY

100 B.C.—*July 12:* Gaius Julius Caesar is born in Rome.

85 B.C.—Caesar's father dies; Caesar puts on the toga and enters manhood.

84 B.C.—Caesar marries Cornelia, daughter of the consul Cinna.

82 B.C.—Sulla returns to power; Caesar refuses to divorce Cornelia and goes into hiding.

80 B.C.—Caesar serves the governor of Asia; earns the "citizen's crown" for bravery in battle.

77 B.C.—Wins respect as a public prosecutor in Rome.
–76

75 B.C.—Ransomed by pirates during a voyage to Rhodes.

69 B.C.—Elected a quaestor and serves in Further Spain.

66 B.C.—Elected curator of the Appian Way.

65 B.C.—Serves as an aedile.

63 B.C.—Elected pontifex maximus, Rome's high priest; also elected a praetor, a high judge.

61 B.C.—Serves as governor of Further Spain.

60 B.C.—Forms the Triumvirate with Pompey and Crassus and is elected consul.

59 B.C.—Serves as consul, forcing through the land bill and other laws.

58 B.C.—Begins career as provincial governor of three provinces and military general; in Gaul, conquers the Helvetii and Germans led by King Ariovistus.

57 B.C.—Conquers the Nervii and the Aduatuci.

56 B.C.—Renews alliance with Pompey and Crassus.

55 B.C.—Defeats the Veneti in a great sea battle; destroys the Usipetes and Tencteri German tribes; builds a bridge across the Rhine River and conducts a raid in Germany; conducts a raid into Britain.

54 B.C.—Conducts second invasion of Britain; puts down rebellion in Gaul.

53 B.C.—Crassus dies at the Battle of Carrhae in the Syrian desert.

52 B.C.—Caesar defeats Gallic king Vercingetorix at Alesia; writes *The Gallic War*.

49 B.C.—*January 10:* Crosses the Rubicon River, in defiance of the Senate, starting civil war.

49 B.C.—*February:* Captures Corfinium.

49 B.C.—*August:* Defeats republican army at Ilerda, Spain.

48 B.C.—*July:* Defeated by Pompey at Dyrrachium, Greece.

48 B.C.—*August 9:* Defeats Pompey at Pharsalus, Greece.

48 B.C.—*September:* Pompey is murdered in Alexandria, Egypt.

48 B.C.—*October:* Caesar lands in Alexandria and chooses to side with Queen Cleopatra in the Egyptian civil war.

47 B.C.—*March 27:* Army of King Ptolemy XIII is defeated.

47 B.C.—*August 2:* Defeats Pharnaces at Zela in Pontus.

46 B.C.—*April 6:* Defeats republican army at Thapsus in Africa.

46 B.C.—*September:* Named Roman dictator for ten years; begins designing social programs to employ Romans and improve their lives.

45 B.C.—Puts down revolt in Spain.

44 B.C.—*February 14:* Voted dictator for life by the Senate.

44 B.C.—*March 15:* Assassinated in the Senate.

CHAPTER NOTES

CHAPTER 1. CROSSING THE RUBICON

1. Christian Meier, *Caesar* (New York: Basic Books, 1982), p. 3.

2. Naphtali Lewis, *The Ides of March* (Sanibel, Fla.: Samuel Stevens & Company, 1984), p. 22.

3. Tom Holland, *Rubicon* (New York: Doubleday, 2003), p. xiv.

4. Arthur D. Kahn, *The Education of Julius Caesar* (New York: Schocken Books, 1986), p. 321.

CHAPTER 2. A ROMAN CHILDHOOD

1. Michael Parenti, *The Assassination of Julius Caesar* (New York: The New Press, 2003), p. 16.

2. Ibid., p. 54.

3. Arthur D. Kahn, *The Education of Julius Caesar* (New York: Schocken Books, 1986), p. 24.

4. Christian Meier, *Caesar* (New York: Basic Books, 1982), p. 57.

5. *Plutarch's Lives*, Vol. 2 (New York: Modern Library, 1992), p. 211.

6. Kahn, p. 51.

Chapter 3. The Young Patrician

1. Michael Grant, *Julius Caesar* (New York: M. Evans & Company, Inc., 1969), pp. 6–7.

2. Arthur D. Kahn, *The Education of Julius Caesar* (New York: Schocken Books, 1986), p. 60.

3. Plutarch, "Caesar," *The Internet Classics Archive*, p. 2, n. d., <http://classics.mit.edu/Plutarch/caesar.html> (May 6, 2005).

4. *Plutarch's Lives,* Vol. 2 (New York: Modern Library, 1992), p. 200.

5. Ibid.

6. Suetonius, *The Lives of the Twelve Caesars* (New York: The Heritage Press, 1965), pp. 50–51.

7. Kahn, p. 89.

8. Naphtali Lewis, *The Ides of March* (Sanibel, Fla.: Samuel Stevens & Company, 1984), p. 6.

9. Ibid.

10. Ramon L. Jimenez, *Caesar Against the Celts* (New York: Sarpedon, 1996), p. 15.

11. Tom Holland, *Rubicon* (New York: Doubleday, 2003), p. 138.

12. *Plutarch's Lives*, p. 206.

13. Kahn, p. 113.

14. Suetonius, p. 8.

15. *Plutarch's Lives,* p. 203.

Chapter 4. Senator and Consul

1. Tom Holland, *Rubicon* (New York: Doubleday, 2003), p. 194.

2. Michael Parenti, *The Assassination of Julius Caesar* (New York: The New Press, 2003), p. 95.

3. Ibid., p. 106.

4. *Plutarch's Lives*, Vol. 2 (New York: Modern Library, 1992), p. 205.

5. Ibid., p. 206.

6. Holland, p. 206.

7. Michael Grant, *Julius Caesar* (New York: M. Evans & Company, Inc., 1969), pp. 25–26.

8. Arthur D. Kahn, *The Education of Julius Caesar* (New York: Schocken Books, 1986), p. 186.

9. Christian Meier, *Caesar* (New York: Basic Books, 1982), p. 182.

10. Grant, p. 30.

11. Suetonius, *The Lives of the Twelve Caesars* (New York: The Heritage Press, 1965), p. 13.

12. Kahn, pp. 194–195.

13. Holland, p. 219.

14. Ramon L. Jimenez, *Caesar Against the Celts* (New York: Sarpedon, 1996), p. 23.

15. Holland, p. 221.

16. Naphtali Lewis, *The Ides of March* (Sanibel, Fla.: Samuel Stevens & Company, 1984), p. 5.

17. Suetonius, p. 14.

18. Meier, p. 218.

CHAPTER 5. PROVINCIAL GOVERNOR

1. Ramon L. Jimenez, *Caesar Against the Celts* (New York: Sarpedon, 1996), p. 30.

2. Julius Caesar, *Caesar's Gallic War*, trans. Joseph Paul (Great Neck, N.Y.: Barron's Educational Series, Inc., 1962), p. 194.

3. Caesar, p. 2.

4. Ibid., p. 7.

5. Ibid., p. 10.

6. Ibid., p. 22.

7. Ibid., p. 29.

8. Ibid., p. 44.

9. Arthur D. Kahn, *The Education of Julius Caesar* (New York: Schocken Books, 1986), p. 233.

10. Jimenez, p. 61.

11. Caesar, p. 49.

12. Meier, p. 246.

13. Jimenez, p. 67.

14. *Plutarch's Lives*, Vol. 2 (New York: Modern Library, 1992), p. 213.

15. Caesar, p. 68.

16. Jimenez, p. 72.

17. Meier, pp. 249–250.

18. Jimenez, p. 74.

19. Anthony Everitt, *Cicero* (New York: Random House, 2001), p. 149.

20. Kahn, p. 249.

CHAPTER 6. GAULS, GERMANS, AND BRITONS

1. Julius Caesar, *Caesar's Gallic War*, trans. Joseph Paul (Great Neck, N.Y.: Barron's Educational Series, Inc., 1962), p. 84.

2. Ibid., p. 113.

3. Ibid., p. 117.

4. Ibid.

5. Ibid., p. 122.

6. Ibid., pp. 122–123.

7. Ibid., p. 123.

8. Ibid., p. 147.

9. Ibid., p. 150.

10. Arthur D. Kahn, *The Education of Julius Caesar* (New York: Schocken Books, 1986), p. 269.

11. Christian Meier, *Caesar* (New York: Basic Books, 1982), p. 295.

12. Caesar, p. 173.

13. Ibid., p. 174.

CHAPTER 7. THE CONQUEST OF GAUL

1. Arthur D. Kahn, *The Education of Julius Caesar* (New York: Schocken Books, 1986), pp. 282–283.

2. Julius Caesar, *Caesar's Gallic War*, trans. Joseph Paul (Great Neck, N.Y.: Barron's Educational Series, Inc., 1962), p. 221.

3. Ibid., p. 239.

4. Ibid., pp. 242–243.

5. Ibid., p. 261.

6. Kahn, p. 289.

7. Caesar, p. 277.

8. Ramon L. Jimenez, *Caesar Against the Celts* (New York: Sarpedon, 1996), p. 186.

9. Caesar, p. 288.

10. Ibid., p. 294.

11. *Plutarch's Lives*, Vol. 2 (New York: Modern Library, 1992), p. 218.

12. Jimenez, p. 188.

13. Christian Meier, *Caesar* (New York: Basic Books, 1982), p. 327.

14. Jimenez, p. 63.

15. Meier, p. 302.

16. Michael Grant, *Julius Caesar* (New York: M. Evans & Company, Inc., 1969), p. 86.

17. Plutarch, "Caesar," *The Internet Classics Archive*, p. 7, n.d., <http://classics.mit.edu/Plutarch/caesar.html> (May 6, 2005).

18. Meier, p. 57.

19. Kahn, p. 296.

20. Meier, p. 236.

21. Kahn, p. 297.

CHAPTER 8. CIVIL WAR

1. Arthur D. Kahn, *The Education of Julius Caesar* (New York: Schocken Books, 1986), p. 313.

2. Anthony Everitt, *Cicero* (New York: Random House, 2001), p. 187.

3. Christian Meier, *Caesar* (New York: Basic Books, 1982), p. 416.

4. Naphtali Lewis, *The Ides of March* (Sanibel, Fla.: Samuel Stevens & Company, 1984), pp. 21–22.

5. Kahn, p. 322.

6. Ibid., p. 323.

7. Tom Holland, *Rubicon* (New York: Doubleday, 2003), p. 293.

8. Michael Grant, *Julius Caesar* (New York: M. Evans & Company, Inc., 1969), p. 104.

9. Holland, p. 307.

10. Julius Caesar, *Caesar's War Commentaries*, ed. John Warrington (New York: E. P. Dutton & Co., Inc., 1958), p. 225.

11. Kahn, p. 349.

12. *Plutarch's Lives*, Vol. 2 (New York: Modern Library, 1992), p. 225.

13. Julius Caesar, *Caesar's Gallic War*, trans. Joseph Paul (Great Neck, N.Y.: Barron's Educational Series, Inc., 1962), p. 205.

14. *Caesar's War Commentaries*, p. 271.

15. Ibid., p. 272.

16. Ibid., p. 283.

17. Everitt, p. 218.

18. *Caesar's War Commentaries*, p. 290.

19. Ibid., p. 292.

20. *Plutarch's Lives,* p. 229.

21. Ibid.

22. Suetonius, *The Lives of the Twelve Caesars* (New York: The Heritage Press, 1965), p. 23.

23. *Plutarch's Lives*, p. 231.

24. Everitt, p. 225.

25. Michael Parenti, *The Assassination of Julius Caesar* (New York: The New Press, 2003), p. 154.

26. T. R. Reid, "The Power and the Glory of the Roman Empire, Part One The Making of an Empire," *National Geographic*, July 1997, p. 24.

27. Kahn, p. 388.

28. Suetonius, p. 44.

29. *Plutarch's Lives,* p. 233.

30. Meier, p. 423.

31. Suetonius, p. 34.

Chapter 9. Dictator

1. Michael Grant, *Julius Caesar* (New York: M. Evans & Company, Inc., 1969), p. 137.

2. Christian Meier, *Caesar* (New York: Basic Books, 1982), p. 443.

3. Ibid., p. 431.

4. Arthur D. Kahn, *The Education of Julius Caesar* (New York: Schocken Books, 1986), p. 406.

5. *Plutarch's Lives*, Vol. 2 (New York: Modern Library, 1992), p. 235.

6. Grant, p. 141.

7. *Plutarch's Lives*, p. 235.

8. Ramon L. Jimenez, *Caesar Against the Celts* (New York: Sarpedon, 1996), p. 215.

9. Grant, p. 145.

10. Suetonius, *The Lives of the Twelve Caesars* (New York: The Heritage Press, 1965), p. 54.

11. Grant, p. 146.

CHAPTER 10. THE IDES OF MARCH

1. Christian Meier, *Caesar* (New York: Basic Books, 1982), p. 428.

2. *Plutarch's Lives*, Vol. 2 (New York: Modern Library, 1992), p. 889.

3. Anthony Everitt, *Cicero* (New York: Random House, 2001), p. 265.

4. Naphtali Lewis, *The Ides of March* (Sanibel, Fla.: Samuel Stevens & Company, 1984), pp. 60–61.

5. Michael Parenti, *The Assassination of Julius Caesar* (New York: The New Press, 2003), p. 175.

6. Meier, p. 485.

7. *Plutarch's Lives,* p. 240.

8. Suetonius, *The Lives of the Twelve Caesars* (New York: The Heritage Press, 1965), p. 58.

9. Plutarch's Lives, p. 241.

10. Tom Holland, *Rubicon* (New York: Doubleday, 2003), p. 335.

11. Suetonius, p. 59.

12. Ibid.

13. *Plutarch's Lives*, p. 242.

14. Holland, p. 336.

15. Lewis, p. 76.

16. Arthur D. Kahn, *The Education of Julius Caesar* (New York: Schocken Books, 1986), p. 446.

17. Lewis, p. 92.

18. William Shakespeare, *Shakespeare The Complete Works*, ed. G. B. Harrison (New York: Harcourt, Brace & World, Inc., 1968), p. 832.

19. Kahn, p. 447.

20. Parenti, p. 185.

CHAPTER 11. THE RISE OF AUGUSTUS

1. Anthony Everitt, *Cicero* (New York: Random House, 2001), p. 267.

2. Naphtali Lewis, *The Ides of March* (Sanibel, Fla.: Samuel Stevens & Company, 1984), p. 137.

3. *Plutarch's Lives*, Vol. 2 (New York: Modern Library, 1992), p. 244.

4. Suetonius, *The Lives of the Twelve Caesars* (New York: The Heritage Press, 1965), p. 64.

5. *Plutarch's Lives*, p. 236.

GLOSSARY

ARTILLERY—Military machines designed to fire missiles.

BATTALION—A body of troops.

BUFFET—To batter or strike.

CATAPULT—A military machine designed to hurl missiles.

GALLERY—A roofed walkway or a room or building used for the display of works of art.

LOTS—Objects used as counters in determining a question of chance.

PAPYRUS—A marsh plant of the Nile River Valley, the soft part of which can be stripped and pressed into a paper-like substance.

PONTIFICE—A member of a council of priests in ancient Rome.

PYRE—A heap of material on which a body can be burned.

REPUBLIC—A government in which voting citizens hold the power to elect representatives and make laws.

TRIBUNE—An elected Roman official with the power to defend the rights of the common people.

TUNIC—A loose article of clothing worn on the upper body and belted at the waist.

VALOR—Strength of mind or spirit; personal bravery.

VETO—The power to refuse.

FURTHER READING

BOOKS

Barter, James. *Julius Caesar and Ancient Rome in World History*. Berkeley Heights, N.J.: Enslow Publishers, 2001.

Everitt, Anthony. *Cicero: The Life and Times of Rome's Greatest Politician*. New York: Random House, Inc., 2002.

Holland, Tom. *Rubicon: The Last Years of the Roman Republic*. New York: Doubleday & Company, Inc., 2004.

Nardo, Don, ed. *Words of the Ancient Romans: Primary Sources*. San Diego, Calif.: Lucent Books, 2003.

INTERNET ADDRESSES

GAIUS JULIUS CAESAR (100–44 B.C.)
<http://www.roman-empire.net/republic/caesar.html>

JULIUS CAESAR CROSSES THE RUBICON
<http://www.eyewitnesstohistory.com/caesar.htm>

JULIUS CAESAR HISTORICAL BACKGROUND
<http://www.vroma.org/~bmcmanus/caesar.html>

INDEX